PUBS OF IN SCOTL

INTRODUCTION

The pub, in Britain, is a national institution. No other nation has succeeded in developing a network of comparable establishments.

On a daily basis, the pub is a social centre at the heart of each local community where friends and acquaintances meet to enjoy a convivial drink or a meal together.

It is also, increasingly, a meeting place for business people, and many an agreement has been reached and finalised over a pint or a gin and tonic.

And many still serve the traditional role of the inn or hostelry; a place offering the traveller comfortable and usually inexpensive accommodation and good food at the end of a day's journey. Though the car may have replaced the horse, the need is still there for a place to rest and be refreshed before the next move.

In compiling this Guide the word 'pub' has been used in a very general sense, and in addition to the traditional pub, includes hotel bars, cafe bars, theme bars etc.

Elsewhere in this publication you can read the interesting story of the evolution of the Scottish pub.

One thing is quite clear however. Other guides published in the United Kingdom have paid scant attention to pubs in Scotland, yet this country has the same rich variety of pubs both rural and urban as has the rest of Britain.

It is the aim of this Guide to bring some of the best of them to your attention.

Pubs, of course, mean different things to different people. The definition of what constitutes a good one is very much a personal judgement. For some, ambience is all important, for others it may be the appeal of a particular Brewer's products, or the quality and variety of food on offer, or the friendliness and standards of the staff.

There will always be those who disagree with the opinion of others. And we all have our own favourite local.

Life has become standardised in so many ways. Popular restaurant chains are almost uniformly dull, each a carbon copy of the other. Pubs are not. Hence their appeal.

If variety really is the spice of life, then we have it in abundant measure in the bars and pubs throughout this country.

There is a fine harvest of experience out there for you to enjoy.

Cheers - or *slainte mhath!*

INTRODUCTION	1
CONTENTS	3
SPONSORS	4
HOW TO USE THIS GUIDE	5
THE EVOLUTION OF THE SCOTTISH PUB	6
LICENSING LAW IN SCOTLAND	9
LISTINGS	11
INDEX	104
CREDITS	108

This Guide to Pubs of Taste in Scotland is sponsored by The Scottish Licensed Trade Association.

Its publication has been made possible by the generous support and financial sponsorship of key companies in the trade.

These sponsoring patrons are:

Allied Distillers Ltd

Alloa Brewery Company Ltd

Arthur Bell Distillers

Guinness Brewing G.B.

Matthew Gloag & Son Ltd

Scottish Brewers Ltd

Tennent Caledonian Breweries Ltd

Willis Wrightson Scotland Ltd

HOW TO USE THIS GUIDE

* Establishments are listed in alphabetical order under the nearest town or village

* Island entries are shown alphabetically by island or island group, e.g. Skye or Lewis

* A full list of establishments in alphabetical order by name is shown in the index at the end of the Guide

THE EVOLUTION OF THE SCOTTISH PUBLIC HOUSE

by Charles McMaster, Scottish Brewing Archive

The Scottish public house as we know it today evolved from the older inns which dated back to time immemorial.

From urbanisation and the rise of the wage economy, coupled with the growth of commercial brewing for sale, the older inns began to be supplemented, in the more populous areas at least, by the public house. This, as its name suggests, was merely a dwelling house with some of the rooms opened to the public for the purpose of drinking. These public houses, or 'howffs' or taverns as they became known, became very popular in the 18th and early 19th centuries, being frequented by persons of every social class. Tavern life became quite a feature of the cities and larger towns, as evinced by the works of Burns, Fergusson and many of the Scottish writers of the period.

However, although snug and convivial, such establishments became increasingly frowned on in the more moralistic early Victorian era, as being dens of dissipation, illicit pursuits and moral degeneracy.

Eventually many public houses of this type were swept away under the licensing restrictions and improvement Acts of the mid 19th century, which in addition to imposing strict hours of closing, differentiated between the public houses and the licensed grocer or victualler, with the former being debarred from selling groceries, and the latter from allowing drink to be consumed on the premises. This had the effect of condemning the Scottish public house to being a mere drinking shop.

In mid to late Victorian times, in an attempt to make public houses more respectable, a very different type of establishment emerged, namely the 'Palace Pub'. These were large, opulent, extravagant public houses, built on a grand scale and commonly featuring imposing gantries, elaborately carved woodwork, fine stained glass, and etched mirrors and glazed tilework.

In stark contrast to the older taverns and dram shops, where it had often been difficult for the publican to supervise exactly what was going on in the separate rooms, these new pubs were for the most open, roomy, high ceilinged and well lit, often featuring a central horseshoe or island bar which commanded the entire establishment.

In addition, they were staffed by a veritable army of barmen and waiters. Nevertheless, despite their opulence, the provision of food played little part in the services on offer in these pubs, despite the efforts of the temperance movement to introduce both food and non alcoholic beverages.

The public houses of late Victorian and Edwardian times are generally regarded, both aesthetically and architecturally, as being the apogee of pub design in Scotland, and no readily identifiable style has appeared subsequently, although in the 1930s there were a few isolated yet outstanding examples of the prevailing 'art deco' and 'moderne' styles.

As a result, by the post-Second World War era, the Scottish public house had changed little in fifty years, and was generally unfavourably contrasted with its English counterpart. Most Scottish public houses remained little more than drinking shops, singularly ill-equipped to cope with the new challenges of the brave post-war world: few served food, while women were little catered for: Scottish licensing laws were more restricted than those in England, there being earlier closing and no Sunday opening.

In the post-Second War days there was a general realisation that the Scottish public house was several decades behind the times, but a number of factors militated against a quick solution. For many years it had been the practice that licences in Scotland could only be held by the individual, and licensing courts were extremely reluctant to grant multiple licences, although these were not actually against the law.

Brewery companies saw their primary role as that of wholesalers rather than retailers, and although they were initially reluctant to abandon this role, it soon became obvious that the task of modernising licensed premises was completely beyond the resources of the individual publican.

Plurality of licences gradually became an accepted way of meeting the challenges of the 1950s and 1960s, notably those posed by television.

The brewers began to modernise the public houses they owned, to make them more attractive and more congenial places to visit: bar food began to make an appearance along with lounge bars, comfortable seating, ladies

toilets, piped music and such like. A curb on this expansion, however, was Scotland's archaic licensing laws, and it was as a result of this general dissatisfaction that in the early 1970s the Clayson Committee was entrusted with the task of evaluating the existing system and making recommendations as to how it might be improved. The bulk of these recommendations were eventually accepted, and formed the basis of the Licensing (Scotland) Act of 1976. The main feature of this Act was the extension of evening hours and some Sunday opening, although all day opening became possible Monday to Saturday as a result. The 1976 Act greatly accelerated the existing trend towards modernising and civilising the Scottish public house. Whilst the existing small seven day licence hotels suffered adversely, the distinction between the hotel or restaurant and the public house became much less sharply defined.
Many public houses now saw an increasing part of their trade being the provision of food and the brewery companies themselves were not slow to respond to this trend.
Great emphasis was placed on staff training and hygiene, coupled with the introduction of technical innovations such as freezers and microwaves. Nevertheless, it must be stressed that the major impetus for these developments came through the consumer, both from the indigenous sector and the tourist sector. Not only was there an increasing demand for pub food, it had to be more adventurous, and incorporate wherever possible fresh local produce.
Nouvelle cuisine was introduced, and more health conscious and vegetarian dishes were catered for as a matter of course rather than an exception. But neither were the traditional Scottish dishes neglected either, with smoked salmon, haggis, stovies and the like also being made readily available.
Nowadays the provision of food forms a significant part of the total turnover of the public house. These new initiatives have done much to bring the Scottish public house into the 1990s. No longer is there a disparity between what the pub has to offer in Scotland compared with its English counterpart. Everybody connected with the trade, from the consumer to the publican, from the brewer to the Scottish Tourist Board, has embraced and welcomed this diversification, and nowadays the Scottish public house offers a quality and variety which can match that on offer anywhere in these islands.

LICENSING LAW IN SCOTLAND

Eric W Ridehalgh, Secretary of The Scottish Licensed Trade Association, explains some of the complexities of current Licensing Acts and some of the changes that may take place this year.

This Guide is being prepared whilst amendments are being made to the Licensing (Scotland) Act 1976. It is impossible to predict the final outcome, at this stage, as the Amending Bill is still progressing through Parliament. Hopefully the amendments will be enacted by midsummer.

The Amending Bill contains many administrative changes. However, as far as members of the public are concerned the expected principal change will mean that hotels and public houses in Scotland will have an automatic right to open from 11 am to 11 pm from Monday to Saturday, if the licensee so wishes. At the moment the licensing hours are 11 am to 2.30 pm and 5 pm to 11 pm. Nevertheless some Licensing Boards, and there are 56 in Scotland, do allow licensees to open from 2.30 pm to 5 pm in the afternoon, but each premise has to make a separate application, and the right to grant permission is totally at the discretion of the local Licensing Board.

Licensees also have the opportunity of applying for extended licensing hours prior to 11 am or after 11 pm for a specific reason, but here again the decision to grant or refuse permission rests firmly with the local Licensing Board.

At the moment the licensing hours on Sunday are 12.30 pm to 2.30 pm and 6.30 pm to 11 pm. This may or not be subject to change.

The issue of allowing children into bars for the purpose of having a meal, is also open to possible change, but the issue is of a more controversial nature. At the moment it is illegal for young people under the age of 14 to be in the bar area of licensed premises, and it is also illegal for persons under 18 to purchase alcohol, or have alcohol purchased on their behalf.

In spite of waiting for licensing amendments, it would be wrong to suggest that as far as customers are concerned, the implementation of the Licensing (Scotland) Act 1976 has been anything other than highly successful.

Prior to 1976 all licensed premises closed at 10 pm unless a private function was being organised by an outside body or organisation. There were no other extended hours as a general rule and public houses were not allowed to open on Sunday.

Relaxation of the licensing system in Scotland in 1976 was soon reflected in the improved standards and a more leisurely attitude experienced by the customer. The increased practice of serving food in public houses, particularly at lunchtime, and the wider range of low and non alcohol drinks available, has also attributed to changed attitudes. The improved facilities and higher standards in hotels and public houses are very much reflected in this new Guide.

ABERDEEN

CAFE ICI
150 Union Street
Aberdeen AB1 1QX
Tel: 0224 648100

Aberdeen city centre – main shopping street.
Maybe it is the modern French style of this interesting cafe bar which gives it its distinctly non-Aberdonian name. It is situated in a converted bank building with an impressive granite frontage. The continental type atmosphere provides the centre of Aberdeen with something different and is extremely popular. Coffee and light snacks are served from 9 am throughout the day and the premises are licensed from 11 am to 12 midnight. This bar does not cater for meals, just snack food. A touch of the continent in the buzz of the city centre and a very welcome one.
Welcome Inns

CAMERON'S INN
6 Little Belmont Street
Aberdeen AB1 1JG
Tel: 0224 644487

A large attractive and recently refurbished city centre bar full of character and charm. 'Ma Camerons' as it is affectionately known to locals has stood the test of time well. The traditional atmosphere of the coaching inn is still evident. There is a warm inviting feel to the place and the staff obviously take pride in it. An extensive but keenly priced menu is available from 12 to 3 pm and from 5 to 8 pm. Closed on Sundays.
Proprietor: A S Bruce

CHURCHILLS
13-17 Crown Street
Aberdeen AB1 2HA
Tel: 0224 586916

Located in the heart of the city this traditionally refurbished eating house has an enviable reputation for the choice, quality and value for money of its menu. It has been furnished and carpeted to a high standard. An extensive menu is available both lunchtimes and evenings during the week and all day on Saturdays with generous portions and reasonable prices. The Family Room welcomes children and is especially popular on Sundays when three course lunches are available. Churchills deserves its fine reputation. In almost every respect this is an excellent pub, setting high standards and with an up-market image. A popular venue to enjoy at any time.
Tennents Taverns

FERRYHILL HOUSE HOTEL
Bon Accord Street
Aberdeen AB1 2UA
Tel: 0224 590867

This is an attractive Georgian building just off the city centre with extensive car parking, a beer garden and a children's play area with swings and slide. The immediate impression is of neatness and tidiness set off with colourful tubs of flowers. Predominantly a business clientele at lunchtime when the open buffet is particularly popular. There are two bars and a dining room, and a warm friendly atmosphere throughout. Meals are served from 12 to 2 pm and from 6 pm in the evening. This is a well established hotel in premises with plenty of character. Open fires in the front hall and Glenogle Bar are a welcoming feature in winter. Most bedrooms have private bathrooms and have TV, telephone, and tea making facilities.
Proprietor: D A Snowie

THE GLENTANAR
39 Holburn Street
Aberdeen AB1 6BS
Tel: 0224 589839

A very impressive corner site in Aberdeen's West End, recently modernised to a high standard and exuding a warm friendly atmosphere. An acceptable range of bar snacks is available at lunchtime six days a week, with first class service. The public areas and toilets are maintained in near faultless condition. A well established well run pub which is a credit to the trade.
Proprietors: Messrs Juroszek & Watson

THE GRILL

213 Union Street
Aberdeen AB1 2BA
Tel: 0224 573530

City centre, opposite the Music Hall.
This is a traditional 'mens bar' with a unique oxidised bronze frontage. Inside, the long mahogany counter and veneered mahogany wall panels are offset by a plain white moulded ceiling.

Although basically a standing pub, some seating and tables are provided. The decor dates from 1926 when it is believed the Grill became the first pub in Aberdeen to serve bar lunches. At the same time a sign was hung in the window which said 'No Ladies, Please!' The sign remained until the passing of the Sex Discrimination Act in 1975. This was despite an invasion by female delegates to the Scottish TUC conference in April 1973 who only left after being bought drinks by the male delegates present. Whilst of course ladies are now given a warm welcome, in order to preserve the character and layout of the bar, there is still no provision of ladies toilet facilities. Although bar lunches were discontinued some 40 years ago, a wide choice of appetising snacks is available all the time, together with an extensive range of beers and spirits.
Proprietor: Graham Watson

ABERNETHY

ABERNETHY HOTEL

Abernethy
Perth PH2 9JN
Tel: 073 885 220

From Perth, 8 miles. From Edinburgh, 39 miles. Exit 9 M90 (Bridge of Earn), situated 4 miles south-east on A913 main St Andrews road from Perth.
Warm wood panelling and an open fire are attractive features in the public bar of this old coaching inn. The former stables have been converted into a comfortable and interesting lounge and function suite. The hotel has six comfortable bedrooms with TV, and tea making facilities. Charming dining room seating 40 plus. Meals and snacks served all day (all home-cooking).

The hotel was a stopping point for such eminent people as Sir Walter Scott and Robert Louis Stevenson.
Proprietors: Mr & Mrs R Wallace

AIRDRIE

THE TUDOR HOTEL

Alexander Street
Airdrie ML6 0BD
Tel: 0236 63295

Approaching Coatbridge from Airdrie on the Edinburgh road.
An elegant grill open seven days lunch and dinner, is complemented by quality bar food in the lounge bar every day between 12 and 2 pm. Additionally the Tudor Hotel is well respected in the area for its catering, specialising in weddings and other functions of a like nature. The hotel has 19 bedrooms all with private facilities and the 'budget cost' policy makes the accommodation particularly attractive to tourists and visitors to the area.
Alloa Brewery

ALEXANDRIA

ALEXANDRIA HOTEL

285 Main Street
Alexandria G83 0AY
Tel: 0389 51717

A clean and homely hotel with a comforting worn feel to it. It has a small, somewhat sparsely furnished public bar, and a very attractive lounge bar where lunches are served. Without going overboard, there is a reasonably wide range of good food available. A beer garden seemed to be used primarily for taking photographs of wedding parties but no doubt would also make an agreeable sitting out area on warm summer evenings. A good sized function suite makes this a popular hotel for local social events. Alexandria attracts quite a number of visitors for whom this would be a pleasant place to drop in to, enjoy a meal and chat with the locals.
Proprietor: Graham Wintersgill

ARBROATH

INVERPARK HOTEL

31 Bank Street
Arbroath DD11 1RH
Tel: 0241 73378

The bar of this seaview hotel is a modern extension with a small terraced beer garden and a well maintained car park. The clientele is usually a mix of locals and holidaymakers and the atmosphere is quiet and friendly, though there is music and dancing on occasions in the lounge bar. The menu sticks to the popular demand items but portions are generous and prices reasonable. Lunch meals are available from noon till 1.45 pm and supper dishes from 6 to 8.30 pm. Service is prompt, efficient and friendly. The interior is well furnished and well maintained with faultless toilets.
Proprietors: Dennis & Helen McIntosh

THE OLD BREWHOUSE

3 High Street
Arbroath
Angus DD11 1BH
Tel: 0241 79945

Straight down High Street to waterfront. Old Listed ex Customs & Excise house now a cosy and interesting eating place. Old oak beams, open fires, and even the original stone slab floor in the 'pub'. Part of the quaintness of the Brewhouse comes from a custom of visitors handing over foreign currency which is pinned to the beams, causing great interest to all newcomers and often friendly arguments from 'regulars' trying to decide which currency is not represented. Bar lunches and suppers are excellent value and range from traditional to the unusual – but find out for yourself. A la carte dinners are served in the evening. This is a place of great charm and character with good quality food. One not to be missed.
Proprietors: James & Jean Stewart

SMUGGLERS TAVERN

The Shore
Arbroath DD1 1DD
Tel: 0241 76927

At harbour corner on main entrance to Arbroath (south).
This small attractive family owned lounge has the surprising distinction of being known far and wide for its unique collection of rum. There were over 180 varieties at the last count! The cellar of the 'Smugglers' was the reputed hiding place for the 'Stone of Destiny' which was removed from Westminster Abbey in 1950. There is not a wide range of food but bar lunches are provided with fine Arbroath smokie, salads a speciality. A very well run and well maintained pub with friendly staff and good standards of service.
Proprietors: Alex & Isobel Shand

ARDGAY

LADY ROSS HOTEL

Ardgay
Sutherland
Tel: 086 32 315

The Lady Ross is a good stopping point for motorists on the busy arterial A9. Set well back from the road there is ample parking both front and rear. There are two bars and a cafe restaurant. The hotel has an all day licence and meals and snacks are available from 9.30 am to around 8 pm. During the winter months food may be served in the cafe only. There is a decent range of inexpensive snacks of the type most in demand by the travelling public.
Proprietor: C Mitchell

AUCHENTIBER

THE BLAIR TAVERN

Auchentiber
Kilwinning KA13 7RR
Tel: 0294 85237

A736 from Glasgow 19 miles, from Irvine 6 miles.
These attractive premises stand on the main Glasgow-Irvine road about six miles north of Irvine, with plenty of car parking, a beer garden in summer and a children's play area. The bar is furnished in old farmhouse style. Tables are fairly tightly packed but this is a very popular place for lunch and every inch of space counts. The bar menu is of the standard variety and at normal prevailing prices. Service is good and speedy. There is a separate restaurant serving lunch and evening meals. This is a well-run establishment with good standards and clearly very popular with the locals.
Welcome Inns

AUCHMITHIE

AUCHMITHIE HOTEL

Auchmithie
By Arbroath DD11 5SQ
Tel: 0241 73010

On the coast 4 miles north of Arbroath. This village hotel with bar and restaurant is perched at the top of the cliffs overlooking the enchanting little harbour nestling at their base. The distinguished Scottish painter, MacIntosh Patrick, captured the essential beauty of the location in his painting 'Road to the Harbour at Auchmithie'. That well-known delicacy the Arbroath smokie originated in the village, which featured in a Sir Walter Scott novel as 'Musselcrags', and Robert Burns is reported to have visited there in 1787. Naturally enough, smokies, crab and fresh fish feature prominently in the freshly prepared bar meals at lunchtime and in the evening. There are high teas with home-baking and a la carte dinners in the Lobster Pot Restaurant.
Proprietors: The Watt Family

AUCHTERLESS

THE TOWIE TAVERN

Auchterless
Nr Turriff AB5 8EP
Tel: 08884 201

On A947 Aberdeen-Banff road (4 miles Fyvie Castle, 4 miles Turriff).
A very rural looking and most appealing family run hotel in an area with interesting places to visit nearby. It is warm and full of character inside with paintings and ornaments decorating all the walls. Quality has been a watchword here and is evident in the style and standard of food presentation. The extensive menu is not cheap but it does represent good value for money. A daily 'Towie Treats' blackboard features fresh fish, shellfish etc depending on availability. Restaurant dinners are served from 6.30 to 9 pm Tuesday to Saturday (later on Saturday) and special family lunches and suppers (5 to 7.30 pm) feature on Sundays. It is advisable to book.
Proprietors: Douglas & Eileen Pearson

AVIEMORE

THE WINKING OWL

Grampian Road
Aviemore
Inverness-shire PH22 1RH
Tel: 0479 810646

From the Police Station, 100 yards, towards north end of village.
Aviemore is a stopping-off place for almost everyone going north to Inverness, and a holiday destination for many others. The Winking Owl is an attractive privately owned and managed pub (alongside the separate a la carte restaurant) long established, and converted from an old crofthouse. Internally it is split level with nooks and crannies and a warm and pleasant atmosphere. The pine-clad ceilings and walls add to the cosy feel of this family pub, locally renowned for good food, service and value, and specialising in malt whiskies and real ale. The garden at the front is very popular during the summer for lunch and/or a quiet

drink and there is a large car park for around 40 cars. The Nest Bar has a good range of snack dishes all modestly priced and representing good value. There is also a children's menu. The staff are attentive but not pushy. seem to enjoy themselves and are anxious that you should do the same.

Proprietors: Mr & Mrs W P McConachie & Partners

AYR

PIERINO'S RISTORANTE & COCKTAIL BAR

1A Alloway Place
Ayr KA7 2AA
Tel: 0292 269087

At the corner of Wellington Square. "A distinct credit to the trade" said our inspector's report, and indeed Pierino's Restaurant and Cocktail Bar is luxurious in the best of Italian taste. The sort of place in which the smart and fashionable like to be seen. Food from an extensive menu is available all day long with a particularly good range of Italian dishes in the evening. Wines are inexpensive and the house wine is particularly good value. Like most family run restaurants it is warm and friendly and the staff give the impression of really enjoying looking after you. Recently refurbished to a high standard Pierino's is likely to make an increasingly important contribution to the culinary scene in Ayr.

Proprietors: Piero & Luisa Vannucci

THE RIVERSIDE INN

By Ayr
Ayrshire KA6 6BW
Tel: 0292 45312

As its name suggests, the Riverside stands on the main road (A77) near the River Doon and has extensive car parking facilities. It caters for both locals and passing holiday-makers. It has earned a good reputation for its food which is available all day from an extensive and very reasonably priced menu. The standard of service is excellent. The staff look competent and professional and no matter how busy they are they take time to welcome customers warmly and to make polite conversation. This is a place that almost everyone would enjoy and which does much to maintain the image of the Scottish pub.

Proprietors: Mr & Mrs N Harper

BALERNO

MARCHBANK HOTEL

Mansfield Road
Balerno
Midlothian EH14 7JT
Tel: 031 449 3970

A long driveway from the main road leads to the former Marchbank House from which this hotel has been converted. It is situated on the outskirts of Balerno in the foothills of the Pentland Hills in a heavily wooded estate. The Marchbank is fundamentally a bar restaurant and while you will be welcomed for a drink you ought really to go for an evening out to dine. The quality of the food is excellent. Tasty bar meals, including delicious open sandwiches served on home-made brown bread are available at lunchtime and in the evening seven days a week. There is also an extensive traditional a la carte menu in the restaurant. A large range of malt whisky, cask conditioned ales, lagers etc are served from the unique barrel fronted bar and families are welcome. This is a well-run, tasteful establishment of high standard.

Proprietors: Mr & Mrs D F Ferguson

BALINTORE

BALINTORE HOTEL

Balintore
Fearn
Ross-shire IV20 1UA
Tel: 086 283 2219/2658

Just off A9, on B9166.
Balintore is a popular centre for sea fishing and indeed is on the north east fishing heritage trail. The Balintore Hotel is a pleasant old house overlooking the Moray Firth and harbour, and with a large out-

door garden area from which to view the mountains and seascape. There is a pleasant split level bar with access to an informal lounge dining room with a further restaurant for more formal occasions. The menu does not go over the top but provides the range of popular demand items and is not over priced. Brass top tables give a smart appearance to the public area. Bedrooms have private bathrooms or showers. Colour TV, tea making facilities etc are also provided.
Proprietors: Keith & Jo Redworth

BALLOCH

THE BALLOCH HOTEL
Balloch Road
Balloch G83 8LQ
Tel: 03895 2579

In the village of Balloch at the south end of Loch Lomond, standing on the north bank of the River Leven. Open all year round, Balloch Hotel really comes into its own during the summer months when tourists and day visitors arrive at Loch Lomond, perhaps the most famous inland loch in the world. The recently refurbished restaurant caters to a high standard and complements the bar food operation which is available all day during the summer, but sticks closer to accepted meal times (12 to 2.30 pm and 5 to 8.30 pm) during the winter months. Twelve letting bedrooms provide a high standard of accommodation, all rooms with private facilities for overnight stay guests.
Alloa Brewery

BANCHORY

POTARCH HOTEL
Kincardine o'Neil
By Banchory
Royal Deeside AB3 4BD
Tel: 03398 84339

There can be few who have not heard of Royal Deeside, so loved by Queen Victoria - and Potarch is in the heart of it. There has been an inn here for 250 years and it must be steeped in much of the history of the area. The Potarch has oak beams, low ceilings many wall ornaments and pictures, and a cheerful open coal fire. Food is available in both bars at lunchtime and in the evening and there is a separate dining room with a more extensive menu. Public areas and toilets are kept in excellent condition. Several of the bedrooms have en suite bathrooms, and all have colour TV and tea making facilities. There are two intriguing stones outside the hotel where horses used to be tethered. Over a drink, ask about them and hear the story of Donald Dinnie!
Proprietors: Messrs Spence & Boyle

BEAULY

LOVAT ARMS HOTEL
High Street
Beauly
Inverness-shire IV4 7BS
Tel: 0463 782313

In this area of great natural beauty this is a gracious 'B' Listed building which sits on the south side of Beauly village square. Log fires welcome you on cooler days. There is a lovely open plan entrance hall and comfortable seating to encourage you to relax. A cocktail bar and dining room off the foyer offer a fine selection of bar food and more formal meals. The staff are well trained, helpful and friendly. Twenty two charming bedrooms, all bathrooms en suite, tea/coffee making facilities and TV. The Lovat Arms is an ideal centre for your golfing, walking or touring holiday. Run by the Fraser family in the centre of Fraser country you can be pretty certain that you will be well looked after.
Proprietors: The Fraser Family

I'VE GOT MINE.

Tennent's Lager

WARSTEINER

The <u>true</u> taste of real German bier

Now available throughout Scotland on draught and in bottles and cans.

The Willis Wrightson approach in Scotland

For the Willis Wrightson approach contact:

160 West George Street, Glasgow G2 2HQ. Telephone Glasgow (041) 332 9655
285 Queen Street, Broughty Ferry, Dundee DD5 2HD. Telephone Dundee (0382) 7379621
31 Drumsheugh Gardens, Edinburgh EH3 7RN. Telephone Edinburgh (031) 225 5333
46 Queen's Road, Aberdeen AB1 6YE. Telephone Aberdeen (0224) 321115

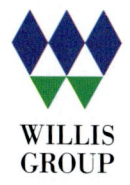

WILLIS GROUP

PEPSI

THE TASTE OF AMERICA

Dewar's Scotch Whisky. It never varies.

Selected Imported Beers. Wines & Spirits.

**BRAND DEVELOPERS
AND WHOLESALERS
TO THE LICENSED TRADE.**

MARBLEHEAD
MARKETING AND BRAND DEVELOPMENT

MARBLEHEAD TRADING LIMITED,
REGISTERED OFFICE: HAWTHORN HOUSE, CLOBERFIELD INDUSTRIAL ESTATE,
MILNGAVIE, GLASGOW G62 7LN, SCOTLAND.
TELEPHONE 041-956 5000   TELEX NO. 779508 MARBLE G   FAX NO. 041-956 6345

Reasons to be Cheerfuel

with Gas

Dundee cake to salmon steak Chefs with class, Insist on Gas..

To find out why contact Industrial and Commercial Sales on 031-559 5000

British Gas Scotland
ENERGY IS OUR BUSINESS

FOR THE BEST AFTER SALES SERVICE IN SCOTLAND

TELEPHONE   **041-613 1119**

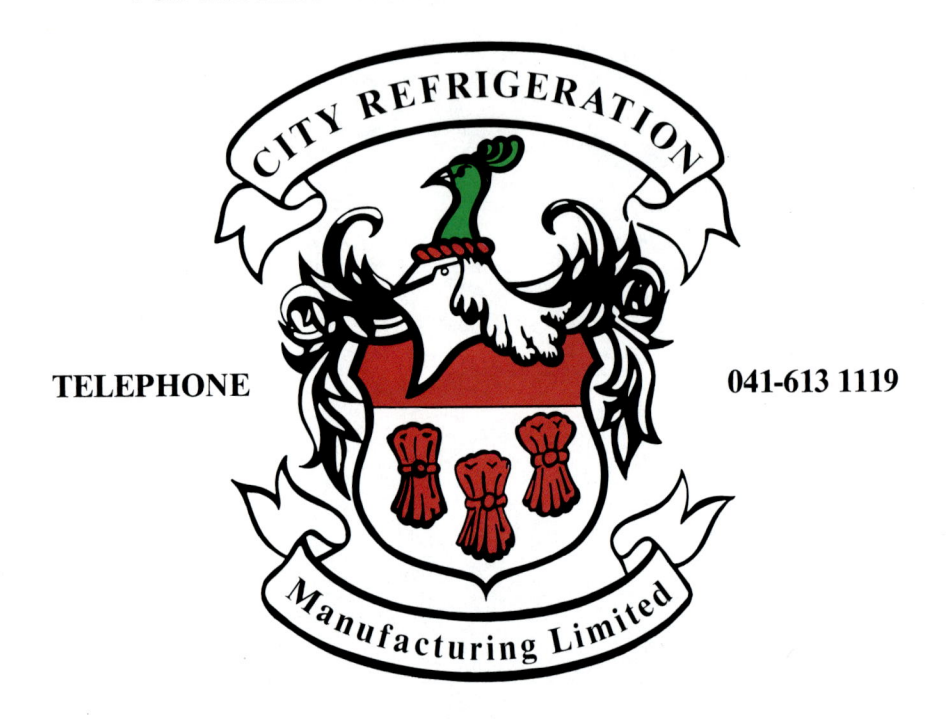

CITY REFRIGERATION (Glasgow) LTD.

GLASGOW - EDINBURGH - ABERDEEN

SALES & SERVICE
"SPECIALISTS TO THE LICENSED TRADE"

GAMKO DISTRIBUTORS

Suppliers of:

★ BEER CELLAR COOLING EQUIPMENT
★ BOTTLE COOLING CABINETS
★ ICE MAKERS
★ FRIDGE FREEZERS

24 Hour Service
Our Telephones are manned from 9.00am-12.00pm 7 Days a Week

PRIORY HOTEL
The Square
Beauly
Inverness-shire IV4 7BX
Tel: 0463 782309

A favourite halt for travellers on the old A9. The Priory is a bustling local hotel with a well deserved reputation for particularly good food and friendly, efficient service. Meals and snacks are available at all times of the day. It is situated in the main square in Beauly close to the ancient Priory ruins that gave the hotel its name, and there is ample parking in the square and some nice shops to browse through. All bedrooms are en suite and fully equipped with TV, trouser press, tea/coffee making facilities etc. Courteous, well mannered staff do much to create the welcoming feel of this place.
Proprietor: Stuart A Hutton

BENBECULA

DARK ISLAND HOTEL
Liniclate
Isle of Benbecula
Western Isles PA88 5PJ
Tel: 0870 2414

In an island with few hotel bars, this one stands out in marked contrast to the traditional style of others. Its thoroughly modern external lines are continued in the interior decor and sumptuous furnishings. The bar lounge is very popular and well patronised and cheerful local girls deal courteously and efficiently with orders taken at the table. Bar lunches offer exceptional value for money as does the evening bar menu. The hotel is a member of the prestigious Taste of Scotland Scheme and the dining room menu reflects the high standards of that Scheme. Bedrooms are very well appointed and comfortable. All in all this is a well run establishment, an admirable oasis in the stark island landscape.
Proprietor: Dark Island Ltd

BLACKFORD

BLACKFORD INN
Stirling Street
Blackford
Perthshire PH4 1QG
Tel: 076482 336

Blackford is situated just off A9 between Stirling and Perth, just south of Gleneagles and Auchterarder. On entering the village turn right over the humpbacked bridge into Stirling Street. The inn is 300 yards down this road on the left.
This is a delightful old inn, with low timber beamed ceilings, magnificent feature fireplace, and furniture and fittings rescued from the old village church. The inn is extremely popular with locals and tourists alike with resident proprietors Jim Kean and Janey Brown always on hand to offer true Scottish hospitality and make guests feel welcome. A small intimate restaurant provides delicious meals at lunchtimes and evenings with many special features at weekends, and a wine list you just wouldn't expect to find in a village inn. Bar snacks are also available at lunchtime and evenings as are vegetarian dishes. The Blackford has two attic bedrooms, which offer basic, clean and affordable accommodation. This is an exceptionally well run and well maintained pub.
Proprietors: Jim Kean & Janey Brown

BLACKNESS

BLACKNESS INN
Blackness
Linlithgow
West Lothian EH49 7JA
Tel: 0506 834252

Situated on the foreshore off the main Queensferry to Linlithgow road, A904. This two storey whitewashed hostelry in the village square is a popular inn overlooking the busy Firth of Forth. It offers the visitor the choice of either a quiet drink in the public bar or an excellent meal in the lounge bar. The lounge with its oak tables and red upholstered chairs has lots of character. In the winter months the open fires in both

bars makes the inn even more welcoming. Food is available every day until 10 pm. It has four letting bedrooms and residents' lounge. A very pleasant local with good facilities and very well run. Lots of atmosphere especially in the evening.
Alloa Brewery
Tenant: J Slavin

BLADNOCH BY WIGTOWN

FORDBANK COUNTRY HOUSE HOTEL

Bladnoch-By-Wigtown
Newton Stewart
Wigtownshire DG8 9BT
Tel: 09884 2346

Fordbank is set on a hill overlooking a pleasant agricultural valley and the Bladnoch Distillery. There is ample car parking and a beer garden with lovely views. Colourful window boxes in the season give an attractive first impression. The interior has been tastefully decorated and has interesting features such as a miniature picture gallery and a collection of water jugs. The staff are very welcoming and cheerful and take time to chat if you are in the mood, without limiting in any way the speed or efficiency of service. Bar lunches are conventional but delicious and reasonable in price. A full dining room service is available at normal breakfast, lunch and dinner times, and packed lunches can be had on request. This is a lovely place to stay to explore the area and judging from comments in the Visitors Book most people would heartily agree.
Proprietor: C Warwick

BLAIRGOWRIE

ROSEMOUNT GOLF HOTEL

Golf Course Road
Blairgowrie
Perthshire PH10 6LJ
Tel: 0250 2604

South of Blairgowrie, 1 mile, Golf Course Road being clearly signed on both Perth and Coupar Angus roads.

The Golf Hotel is a converted farmhouse on three floors, surrounded by its own gardens, in what has become a very exclusive suburb of Blairgowrie close to the Golf Club and its beautiful Rosemount Course. There are 12 rooms, all with en suite facilities, colour TV, direct dial telephone, tea tray, thermostatic heating controls, electric blankets. The clientele embraces golfers, skiers, sportsmen and just tourists having fun in the heart of Scotland's playground. There are also self-catering chalets to let in the grounds, sleeping six each in comfort. Lunch is served in the lounge bar from a long menu which can be as light or as large as you wish. Traditional Scottish high teas are served in the early evening, followed by table d'hote dinners, but bar suppers are served all evening to 9.45 pm. The wine list is headed by the luscious wines from Rosemount Estate in Hunter Valley, Australia. The Bunker Bar has an extensive range of single malt whiskies as well as a collection of bag-tags from courses all over the world. This is not a pub in the basic sense of that word but it is a lovely place to stay or visit, with many interesting features.
Proprietors: D G & G M Mansion

BLYTH BRIDGE

THE OLD MILL INN

Blyth Bridge
Nr West Linton
Peeblesshire EH46 7DG
Tel: 0721 52220

A701 Edinburgh-Moffat road (21 miles from Edinburgh).
Set in the beautiful Scottish Borders, ten miles from Peebles, the historic (1817) red sandstone Old Mill Inn has retained many of the features of the former cornmill in a lovely bar and restaurant. The Kiln Lounge is especially interesting with its copper sheath fireplace and gleaming horse brasses. A large cartwheel has been formed into a light fitting over the drystone bar. An imaginative a la carte menu is served both lunch and dinner in the restaurant with its lovely old housekeeper's press. A traditional Sunday lunch is also available. Bar meals are served

every day and from spring 1990 the garden will have a courtyard for serving lunchtime meals and to enjoy a leisurely drink. For years this has been a favourite place to drive out to from Edinburgh so it should appeal to just about everyone. Strongly recommended.
Proprietors: Mr & Mrs R Rhatigan

BOWER

THE BOWER INN
Bower
By Wick
Caithness KW1 4TT
Tel: 095 586 292

B876 Thurso-Castletown-Wick: 4 miles from Castletown, 10 miles from Wick.
The Bower has every right to be pleased with itself. It exudes that comfortable homely atmosphere of a real 'local'. It has been tastefully furnished and decorated with a lot of attention to detail, giving it a pleasing relaxing feel. Good home-cooking is evident in the daytime bar snacks. There is emphasis on fresh local produce and this is particularly noticeable in the more formal meals available in the comfortable restaurant. For the figure conscious the Bower claims to offer non-fattening sweets!
Proprietors: R A & A E Budding

BRIDGE OF ORCHY

INVERORAN HOTEL
Nr Bridge of Orchy
Argyll PA36 4AQ
Tel: 083 84 220

Away from the madding crowd, this fine old country hotel in a Highland glen is very popular with walkers on the West Highland Way. Sportsmen and others seeking a quiet retreat also make their stay here. It has been refurbished recently and is tastefully furnished, tidy and welcoming. A limited bar menu is available all through the day and is inexpensive. Non residents are normally limited to the bars unless they have made previous arrangements. There are showers and/or wash basins in the bedrooms. In an area of great natural beauty this would be a good base from which to enjoy some of it.
Tenant: Mrs Janet Blackie

BURNMOUTH

THE FLEMINGTON INN
Burnmouth
Berwickshire TD14 5SL
Tel: 08907 81277/81357

On A1, 5 miles north of Berwick-upon-Tweed.
This has been the 'first and last inn' in Scotland for over two hundred years and was at one time a stopping point for stagecoaches from the north. Burnmouth is a pretty fishing village just off the A1 at the start of the Berwickshire coastal tourist route. It is an attractive detached cottage-style building with whitewashed exterior, pantile roof and hanging flower baskets. This is a compact, cosy and well-run pub catering for locals as well as passing trade. It has good furnishings and is well-maintained and equipped. Bar meals, for lunch or supper, have a good home-cooked quality and represent good value for money. Local produce, including shellfish and salmon, is used as much as possible, and is available seven days a week. Give enough notice and, in season, you may even enjoy local lobster.
Proprietors: Mr & Mrs G R Smillie

BURRELTON

BURRELTON PARK HOTEL

High Street
Burrelton
By Coupar Angus
Perthshire PH13 9NX
Tel: 08287 206

On A94, 12 miles from Perth and 2 miles from Coupar Angus.
Situated in the village of Burrelton, this well cared for property with its hanging baskets and canopies is as pleasant inside as it is outside. It exudes a warmth of hospitality from its proprietor and staff who genuinely care. It is renowned throughout Perthshire, Angus and Fife for its comprehensive imaginative bar meal menu. Bar meals are available from 11 am to 11 pm seven days a week all year round. A la carte meals are served in the restaurant from 7.30 to 10.30 pm. Six en suite bedrooms with colour TV, hostess trays etc. A very definite stopping place on this main north/south arterial road.
Proprietor: E M Weaving

CALLANDER

ROYAL HOTEL

Main Street
Callander
Perthshire FK17 8DU
Tel: 0877 30651/30973

North of Stirling on A84.
Callander of course is the gateway to the Trossachs, that unusually named and ill-defined but most beautiful area of central Scotland. The Royal has an impressive sandstone frontage in the main shopping street. The combination of tourists and locals in the bar help create a good feeling inside. A limited menu has been designed and priced to appeal to patrons and the staff go out of their way to be friendly and welcoming. There is entertainment most weekends. Bedrooms have TV, and tea making facilities.
Tenant : Mr & Mrs R Russell

CARDROSS

CARDROSS INN

Main Street
Cardross
Dunbartonshire G82 5JY
Tel: 0389 841358

Situated in the centre of Cardross village on A814, 2 miles west of Dumbarton and 5 miles from Helensburgh.
A typical local maintained to a high standard. It has an interesting conservatory, a beer garden open during the summer, and good parking. There is a good old fashioned atmosphere about with a steady buzz of conversation. The extensive bar menu has a wide range of simple inexpensive food tailored to the market it serves, which includes children. The restaurant menu features steaks, rainbow trout etc.
Alloa Brewery
Tenant : M Whitfield

CARLUKE

AQUILA'S LOUNGE BAR & RESTAURANT

33 Lanark Road
Braidwood
Carluke ML8 4PW
Tel: 0555 71206

Situated on A73, tourist route going from M74 at Abington towards Stirling, and 1 mile south of Carluke.
This is a completely new building, with beautiful decor and furnishings completed to a very high standard. The lounge bar stocks a good array of Scotch whiskies and there is a warm and friendly atmosphere with caring and attentive staff. There are bar lunches, high teas and bar suppers, served throughout the day until 10 pm. The restaurant caters for family and business lunches and does so to a high standard. There is an adjacent garden centre and tearoom, with good home-baking and where families with young children are catered for with a children's menu. Have the proprietor, Bill 'Baron' Irvine, sign one of his

books of funny poetry for you. As part of a garden centre this is an unusual situation but it looks set to become extremely popular and possibly quite a tourist attraction in the Clyde Valley.
Proprietors: William & Mary Irvine

STATION INN
**Braidwood
Carluke
Lanarkshire ML8 6PD
Tel: 0555 72105**

On A73 road, 5 miles north of Lanark and 1 mile south of Carluke.
Pass through the traditional Scottish public bar to the attractive beer garden and enjoy this inn's excellent home-cooked meals on sunny lunchtimes. Food is also served in the small modern lounge. The Station Inn's high standard of service has been recognised by Alloa Brewery Company who have presented them with a 'Good Beer' Award. This is neither a stuffy nor pretentious pub but it is friendly and well managed and there is a pleasant atmosphere.
**Alloa Brewery
Tenant: Mrs E Kelly**

CARNOCK

THE OLD INN
**6 Main Street
Carnock
Nr Dunfermline
Fife KY12 9JQ
Tel: 0383 850381**

A907 main Stirling-Dunfermline road. 2 miles west of Dunfermline.
A quaint old inn in the rural village of Carnock. It dates back to 1669 and despite considerable modernisation, refurbishment and extension retains many of the original features and much of its charm. Children are made welcome and there is a play area for them at rear of the beer garden. Food is quite inexpensive and there is a surprisingly wide choice. Bar lunches and suppers are available every day including Sunday and there is a 52 seat restaurant with an a la carte menu. A really nice inn with atmosphere, hospitality and good food.
Tenant: Derek & Lorraine Stuart

CARNWATH

WEE BUSH INN
**99 Main Street
Carnwath
Lanarkshire ML11 8HH
Tel: 0555 840 587**

On A721 Ayr-Edinburgh road, 7 miles from the market town of Lanark. From Edinburgh, 35 minutes.
Although England boasts many a thatched pub there are surprisingly few in Scotland and this is a really charming old thatched roof inn at least a couple of hundred years old. Internally it has been very tastefully furnished and the welcome is quick and genuine. Helen Wilson, the proprietor, has a warm and lively personality and the staff take their cue from her and provide an excellent standard of service. There are conventional and modestly priced bar snacks but there is also a remarkably extensive and sophisticated dinner menu with something to titillate even the most jaded palate. This is unquestionably a first class pub with a fine image and an interesting history. If you are in the area don't miss it, but it is also very much a destination to which to drive from anywhere within a 30 mile or so radius.
Proprietor: Helen C Wilson

CARRADALE

CARRADALE HOTEL

Carradale
Argyll PA28 6RY
Tel: 058 33 223

On A842, 9 miles north of Campbeltown, Argyll.

From whichever direction one approaches it the route to Carradale is spectacular. So is the village itself, and especially so is the Carradale Hotel. This is one of those hotels that it is joy to discover. It has been owned and managed by the same family for over 80 years and their warm welcome and caring attitude permeate to every member of staff. It is a splendid well-maintained building in a dominant site with attractive gardens, a new conservatory and two bars. The menu and presentation of the bar food is markedly superior and prices are very moderate. Children are made particularly welcome. Carradale is somewhat off the normal tourist routes but for anyone visiting the Mull of Kintyre this should be a 'must'.

Proprietors: John & Katherine Martin

CASTLECARY

CASTLECARY HOUSE HOTEL

Main Street
Castlecary
Cumbernauld G68 0HD
Tel: 0324 840233

On the B816, which is parallel to A80, going north of Cumbernauld.

This is a small private hotel with 35 comfortable rooms, the majority of which have all facilities. A good standard of lunches and suppers is served in all of the bars, which also offer a fine selection of real ales. The Cameron Restaurant is warm and intimate and offers a varied a la carte menu. On a Sunday, traditional high teas are served. Castlecary is on the site of the Antonine Wall, which is the most important Roman monument remaining in Scotland and can be reached by a path, a short walk from the hotel.

Proprietor: K McMillan

CAWDOR

THE CAWDOR TAVERN

The Lane
Cawdor
Nairn IV12 5XP
Tel: 06677 316/676

Set in the historic conservation village of Cawdor, close to the castle made famous by Shakespeare's *MacBeth* lies this beautiful and tastefully furnished little inn. The lounge bar is panelled in oak and there is a cheerful log fire to greet you on a chilly day. Here the emphasis is on comfort. Even in the function room, which caters for 80, it is difficult to detect a trace of plastic or formica. In summer you can sit on the patio under colourful awnings and enjoy the peace and tranquillity of this beautiful village. There is a wide choice of satisfying meals and vegetarian dishes are available on request. Most dishes are home-made using fresh local produce. Meals are available all year round but evening meals are restricted to weekends only during winter. A lot of thought and attention to detail has gone in to the planning of the Cawdor Inn. This is a gem of a little pub, very successful. Advisable to make a reservation for a meal in advance.

Proprietors: Mr & Mrs Thomas D Oram

CLOVENFORDS

CLOVENFORDS HOTEL

1 Vine Street
Clovenfords
Nr Galashiels TD1 3LU
Tel: 089 685 203

At main crossroads in centre of village of Clovenfords.

A good country pub/hotel with white-washed exterior, catering for locals and visitors alike. A large statue of Sir Walter Scott stands outside this, the village pub. Food is served all day from morning coffee through to bar suppers in the evening. There is also a separate dining room. The standard is unpretentious but value for money. Service from the staff is very good and the whole place has a welcoming atmosphere.

Proprietor: Mrs Maureen Corrie

COMRIE

THE DEIL'S CAULDRON

**Dundas Street
Comrie
Perthshire PH6 2LN
Tel: 0764 70352**

On A85 Perth to Crianlarich road at the west end of Comrie.

For those on their way to or from Crianlarich or Lochearnhead the conservation village of Comrie is a natural stopping-off place. It hasn't changed much over the years and indeed the Deil's Cauldron is a 250 year old Listed building. It stands out well beside its neighbours but is attractively different though the exterior gives little hint of the pleasant changes within. Rough natural stone walls with upholstered bench seating, refectory tables and some stools, provide a comfortable ambience in which to enjoy some of the excellent range of well presented meals and snacks. This is really a bar restaurant concentrating on good food of excellent value both at lunchtime and in the evening. This is a well-maintained well-run establishment which deserves to do well, and the sort of place which Comrie has long needed.

Proprietors : Robert & Judith Shepherd

CONNEL FERRY

FALLS OF LORA HOTEL

**Connel Ferry
By Oban
Argyll PA37 1PB
Tel: 063171 483**

On A85, 5 miles before Oban, 2-3 hours drive north-west of Glasgow or Edinburgh. A handsome and well-kept late Victorian hotel in very tidy gardens and grounds overlooking spectacular scenery of sea and mountains. A good family stopping off place either for a stay or when passing through. The 'pub' here is really the hotel's cocktail bar which with its open log fire and over 100 brands of whisky to tempt you, is a comfortable place in which to relax. Adjoining the bar is a popular and attractive Bistro with an extensive selection of meals or snacks served throughout the day. There are 30 bedrooms from inexpensive family rooms to beautiful luxury rooms – one with a seven foot round bed and an exotic jacuzzi bathroom en suite. The bedrooms are comfortable and tastefully decorated. Oban, with its ferries to the islands is but ten minutes away by car.

Proprietor : Mrs C M Webster

COYLTON

CHERRY TREE HOTEL

**40 Main Street
Coylton
Ayrshire KA6 6JW
Tel: 0292 570312**

The Cherry Tree is a small hotel set in a pleasant terrace on the Main Street. It has been simply and tastefully decorated in country inn style. A good atmosphere in the bar area, where there is an extensive menu. The food is of a very high standard, imaginatively put together and well served. Service is good, the staff being very helpful and welcoming. This pub has all the signs of good management and enhances the image of the pub in Scotland by its excellence, particularly for its food.

Proprietor : Mrs Jacqueline Dowds

CRIEFF

ARDUTHIE HOTEL

**Perth Road
Crieff PH7 3EQ
Tel: 0764 3113**

Just east of town on main Perth-Crieff road. This hotel is set back from the road in its own well-kept grounds, with car parking. Furnished in keeping with the style of the building but clean and smart. Food available in bar, lunch and evenings, good selection, well presented. There is also a separate dining room. The staff of the Arduthie make you feel very welcome and our inspector concluded that he would choose to return here for a quiet repast. A very nice quiet hotel offering good food and hospitality.

Proprietors : John & Noreen Milner

CROFTAMIE

THE WAYFARERS

Croftamie
Glasgow G63 OEU
Tel: 0360 60358

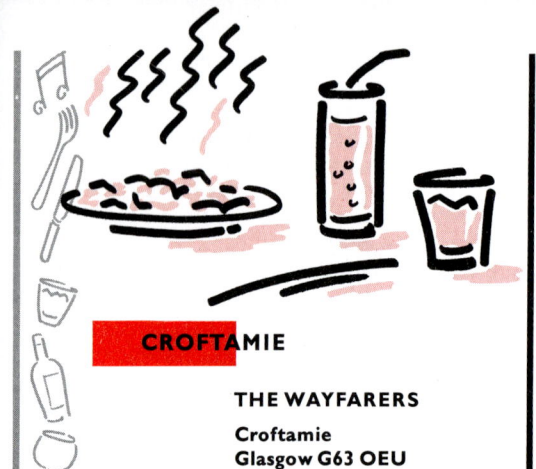

Situated in the village of Croftamie on road A809, 1/2 mile south of the junction with A811 Balloch-Stirling road. Only 1/2 hour's drive from Glasgow.
The Wayfarers is a very attractive inn and is a combination of a village pub, an elegant lounge bar and an up-market cocktail bar, it has been owned by the same family for 30 years. During summer months an attractive veranda and garden come into use, in the winter there is the huge log fire to welcome customers. The reputation of the Wayfarers has been built on friendly, efficient service and value for money. The range of international drinks in general and malt whiskies in particular is particularly good. Buchanan Aitken who is usually behind the bar is involved in the International Bartenders Association, has a wide knowledge of drinking habits in over 30 countries of the world and is happy to chat knowledgeably on the subject. Irene, his wife, is in charge of the food operation which specialises in good home-cooking such as warming wholesome soups, and the famous Wayfarers Pies. Lunch is served from noon till 2 pm and evening meals are served from 6.30 pm in the bar or in the adjoining dining room, The Red House. The Wayfarers is closed on Mondays and during the month of February. This is a place with a lot going for it. Standards everywhere are high, welcome is genuine. A little off the beaten track but well worth making the effort to get there.

Proprietor: Buchanan Aitken

CROMARTY

CROMARTY ARMS

Church Street
Cromarty
Ross-shire IV11 8XA
Tel: 03817 230

Located in the old world part of the village of Cromarty this is a pub that gives an immediately pleasing impression with its lovely hanging baskets of flowers in summer. It has recently been renovated in an attractive nautical theme and the comfortable warm bar is very relaxing. The food is entirely appropriate to the premises and sufficiently varied to appeal to all tastes. Children are welcome and catered for, as are vegetarians. It is apparent from their attitude that the friendly polite staff take pride in this charming little pub, and rightly so. It is altogether very pleasant.

Proprietor: Mrs Marie Clarke

ROYAL HOTEL

Marine Terrace
Cromarty
Ross-shire IV11 8YN
Tel: 03817 217

North-east of Inverness, 20 miles on A832 - the main road on Black Isle.
If you are in the mood to do so you can almost lean out and touch the oil rigs as they pass the front door from the oil rig yard of Nigg, so there is something of unusual interest here. The Royal is a traditional and unpretentious Highland hotel with an extremely good cross-section of customers and high repeat business. Busy, yet relaxing and friendly and representing good value for money. You may eat in the dining room or lounge bar choosing from a decent range of dishes and a menu which particularly caters for children. There are a number of well appointed bedrooms all with private facilities. The hotel notepaper perhaps sums up the place: "Where ye haste to the welcome and prolong the goodbyes".

Proprietors: Stewart & Betty Morrison

DALKEITH

THE JUSTINLEES INN
**Eskbank Toll
Dalkeith
Midlothian EH22 3AT
Tel: 031 663 7644**

Six roads meet at the busy Eskbank Toll where Justinlees is situated. It is an imposing two storey building with a well-maintained look and a large car park to the rear. The pub has recently been extensively renovated inside and the interior is open, spacious and very comfortable. There are lounge bar meals downstairs at lunchtime while the separate Ostlers Restaurant upstairs puts on a wider choice for both lunch and dinner. Ideally situated for passing trade from all directions the Justinlees is also popular with business people and locals, and deservedly so. This is a good pub with high standards.
Welcome Inns

THE SUN INN
**Lothianbridge
Nr Dalkeith
Midlothian EH22 4TR
Tel: 031 663 5800**

Directly on A7 Galashiels road. South of Edinburgh, 7 miles.
This cosy and attractive pub is situated next to Lothianbridge viaduct which carried the former Waverley Line rail link from Edinburgh to Carlisle. It has a large car park and a small outside patio with children's play area. Attractive oak beams in the bar and a wood burning stove give a warm welcoming atmosphere. Good home-cooked food is available from 12 to 9.30 pm weekdays and Sunday lunches and suppers are also served. Excellent value for money, and families are made welcome. Service is speedy and friendly and there is evidence of attention to detail and high standards of cleanliness throughout. A good stopping place for passing motorists and a popular rendezvous for local business people and residents. Five cottage style bedrooms with en suite facilities are due to open in April 1990.

Proprietors: Roy & Sheila Tyldesley

DAVIOT EAST

THE DEERSTALKER LOUNGE BAR & RESTAURANT
**Daviot East
Inverness-shire IV1 2XQ
Tel: 046 385 223**

An old crofters steading converted over the years into a very attractive bar. It is adjacent to a caravan site and has ample car parking and a children's playground. Inside there are original stone walls, open fireplaces, antlers, guns etc creating the character of the place. Furnishing and decor show taste and the skill of exacting craftsmen. There is a restaurant for more formal eating, but the bar lunches offer a sound variety of the popular dishes which most people want. The Deerstalker is best summed up as an attractive friendly little pub and is well worth a visit.

Proprietors: Claude & Helena Ponty

DENNY

HORSEMILL INN
**Woodyett Farm
Denny
Stirlingshire FK6 6BL
Tel: 0324 822241**

This is a nice, pleasant, relaxed country pub. The premises are well laid out, there is ample car parking, good gardens, a beer garden and a children's play area. The interior is welcoming, with oak beams, a large fireplace and good furnishings. The menu is fairly restricted, but that is no bad thing. What there is, is good and generously portioned. There is a separate dining room. Bar food is available till 9.30 pm. Public areas and toilets are kept in neat, clean and tidy condition throughout the day. You should enjoy a visit here either for a social drink or a meal.

Proprietors: Hamish & Margaret Taylor

DINGWALL

THE NATIONAL HOTEL

**High Street
Dingwall
Ross-shire
IV15 9HA
Tel: 0349 62166**

In town centre of Dingwall.
An attractive hotel situated in the centre of the county town of Dingwall, an ideal base for touring the north and west Highlands. The interior is spacious and comfortable with a friendly attentive staff. The Ballantyne Bar features a contemporary imaginative menu which offers excellent value. The special 'kids corner' menu has meals that children like to eat at prices parents like to pay. Bar meals are served at lunch and dinner every day of the year. The hotel has 42 bedrooms, all en suite, and has plenty of free parking. This is a good town centre hotel making every effort to cater well for its varied clientele.
Proprietor : Ross Rahn

DOLLAR

IZZY'S RESTAURANT & WINE BAR

**Lorne Tavern
17 Argyll Street
Dollar, Clackmannanshire
FK14 7AR
Tel: 0259 43423**

A very interesting establishment in an interesting historic village. Izzy's Restaurant and Wine Bar have a lot to offer. Done up in old world style it is small and intimate and the pleasant atmosphere pervading it seems to appeal to all age groups. The restaurant menu, for both lunchtime and evenings, is extensive and of high standard not steep, but good value for money. Jack and Isabelle Currie give a friendly welcome and their standards permeate to the rest of the staff. Not too easy to find – but persist.
Proprietors: Jack & Isabelle Currie

DRUMNADROCHIT

LEWISTON ARMS HOTEL

**Lewiston
Drumnadrochit
Inverness-shire IV3 6UN
Tel: 04562 225**

A long low whitewashed inn which was formerly an old brewery in a quiet backwater just off the Fort William-Inverness road. The gardens behind the hotel sweep down to the river and have one of Scotland's few 'petang' pitches. Local characters give atmosphere to the public bar, and join them if you want to see life – while the lounge bar provides a quiet haven for residents and travellers. There is a limited, but adequate, menu in the bar restaurant. Children are welcome and in good weather it is enjoyable to eat out in the garden. This is not a pretentious place. It is an honest to goodness pub and our inspector summed it up neatly by saying "If you didn't get a warm welcome I am sure you would get your money back."
Proprietors: N J & H W Quinn

DRUMOAK

THE IRVINE ARMS/ GEORDIES BYRE

**North Deeside Road
Drumoak AB3 3AV
Tel: 03308 423**

On A93, 3 miles west of Peterculter.
This unique bar won a Guinness Design Award of Excellence. It is fitted out as a milking parlour complete with cattle stalls, milk churns and bar stools, sacks of grain and many authentic touches. The comfortable lounge which has been tastefully refurbished boasts an open fire in the cooler weather. Excellent home-cooked meals are served in the bar or lounge at sensible prices. Lunch 12 till 2 pm and supper 6.30 to 8.30 pm seven days.
Proprietors: George & Claire Wight

DUFFTOWN

A TASTE OF SPEYSIDE
10 Balvenie Street
Dufftown
Banffshire AB5 4AB
Tel: 0340 20860

Just off the square on the Craigellachie road. A small family run pub/restaurant specialising in local food and Speyside malt whisky. A good central base for visitors to local distilleries. Interesting displays of local food and whisky and a unique information service with details of over 40 Speyside distilleries that welcome visitors. Maybe the world's best selection of Speyside malts including many old and rare whiskies dating back to 1948. Food specialities include locally smoked salmon and venison, farmhouse cowsmilk and goatsmilk cheeses. Home-made pates, Aberdeen Angus steak and home-made wholemeal bread. Winner in 1988 of the Taste of Scotland/Caithness Glass Prestige Award for the best bar lunch. Open from 11 am to 9 pm daily but closed in January and February. A simple and unpretentious pub restaurant but not likely to let you down.
Proprietors: Ann McLean & Joe Thompson

DUMFRIES

THE FIVE ARCHES
345 Annan Road
Dumfries DG1 3JR
Tel: 0387 64328

On A75 in Dumfries.
This appropriately named red brick building with its five arches stands on the main Carlisle-Stranraer road on the outskirts of Dumfries. With tubs of flowers and hanging baskets it has a well-kept look and there is ample car parking. This is a popular pub, catering for locals, business people and tourists. Disco functions can make it somewhat noisy some nights – but not with the young patrons who are enjoying them. The food is straightforward and unpretentious - and good value for money. Bar lunches served between 12 and 2 pm and bar suppers 6.30 to 8.30 pm. There is a patio with rustic seating for summer days and evenings. Children are welcome.
Proprietors: Mr & Mrs Ayre & Family

THE FLESHERS ARMS
48 Loreburn Street
Dumfries DG1 1HN
Tel: 0387 56461

A very busy town centre pub, popular with all age groups by day but tending towards a younger clientele in the evening. It has been completely refurbished in Victorian style and has a fine collection of old golf clubs, pewter jugs and old stone bottles. A limited snack menu is served most of the day in the bar with delicious home-made soup and a range of filled rolls, sandwiches etc. There is a lively atmosphere about this excellent bar, the public areas of which are maintained to a high standard.
Proprietors: Mr & Mrs J Thomson

GLOBE INN
56 High Street
Dumfries DG1 2JA
Tel: 0387 52335

You do not need to be a Burns enthusiast to appreciate the Globe, but the spirit of Rabbie Burns almost speaks to you here where he spent so many happy evenings. This is a place full of character and virtually unchanged over the last 200 years. Tucked away in a narrow alley off the High Street, the Snug Bar is a fine example of an old 'howff' which has been carefully and lovingly preserved, still retaining much of the beautiful old wood panelling that was there when Burns occupied his favourite seat by the fireplace. A lot of good fresh local produce is featured on the menu both in the lounge bar and the dining room. For its historical connection alone the Globe is well worth a visit, but there is more to it than that. This is a bit of old Scotland steeped in folklore and certainly worth a couple of hours of anyone's time. A visit to Dumfries will be incomplete without a visit to the Globe.
Proprietor: Globe Inn Ltd

QUEENS HOTEL

**Main Road
Locharbriggs
Dumfries DG1 3NU
Tel: 0387 710333**

The rather conventional outside appearance of the Queen's gives no indication of some pleasant surprises inside. Alterations and renovation were taking place at the time of our inspector's visit so we do not have the full picture to report, but even so it is clear that standards are high and there is much to commend. There is a charming small dining room with a remarkably good menu representing first class value and served by cheerful attentive staff who seemed to care for their customers and their standards. The bar lunch menu is not excessively extensive but has enough variety to meet the needs of a varied clientele. Portions are good. The proprietors are obviously keen to go on improving this establishment and that augurs well for the future.

Proprietors: Mr & Mrs P Oatridge

QUEENSBERRY HOTEL

**16 English Street
Dumfries DG1 2BT
Tel: 0387 53526**

Town centre.
Right in the heart of Dumfries the Queensberry has a corner site on the edge of the pedestrian precinct some 50 yards from a small car park. It is an old established hotel with a comfortable lounge and a separate dining room. The public bar on the ground floor tends to be busy but upstairs the atmosphere is much more of a family hotel. Food is good and imaginative – more so than one might expect from the exterior of the hotel. Bars are open all day with a good range of snack meals. Bedrooms are well equipped and the majority have private facilities.

Proprietors: J & R J Bradford

RAGGAZZI

**19-21 English Street
Dumfries DG1 2BU
Tel: 0387 55157**

At the fringe of the pedestrianised area, Raggazzi's serves a dual role. By day it is a quiet conventional bistro style establishment, and at night it becomes a busy popular young persons -disco bar. The downstairs bar and dining area are small but decorated and equipped in an attractive modern manner. There is a large lounge area upstairs. The menu specialises in continental filled rolls with side salads and is presented with typical Italian flair. Portions are generous and there was a good housewine at only 85p a glass at the time of our visit. The whole atmosphere of this establishment is good with a very pleasant staff eager to please. Public areas and toilets are maintained in spotlessly clean condition. This is a place to enjoy a delicious light midday meal in delightful surroundings or if you are in the right age group, to enjoy a lively night out.

Proprietor: G M Campanile

ROTCHELL HOTEL

**Corbelly Hill
Dumfries
Tel: 0387 61612**

The Rotchell stands in its own grounds on a hill overlooking Dumfries in an area of good quality housing. It has been tastefully refurbished recently with the bar in traditional Victorian style and an archway and folding door through to the dining area and function room. The menu is conventional and unpretentious but portions are good and customers seem well satisfied. Both lunches and suppers are available in the bar. Public areas are maintained to a high standard as are toilets. This would be a very good venue for a family bar lunch with no doubt a wider ranging clientele in the evening.

Proprietor: Mrs C Potts

TROQUEER ARMS

Troqueer Road
Dumfries
Tel: 0387 54518

A large and imposing building with a car park in front and a beer garden and children's play area at rear. The interior is Victorian in appearance and this goes well with the original corniced ceilings and the general feel of a large house. It is well known locally and draws its clientele from a wide area. Simple snacks are available all day and prices do not come as a shock. A young cheerful staff copes well with the service of food and drink. A lot of attention is given to keeping the public areas clean, neat and tidy. The locals already know about it and it is just the sort of place to satisfy the tourist or visitor looking for a little of the real flavour of Scotland.
Tennents Taverns
Tenant: John Potts

DUNBLANE

STIRLING ARMS HOTEL
Stirling Road
Dunblane
Perthshire FK15 9EP
Tel: 0786 822156

Dunblane has a much better recorded history than most cities of its size with origins going back to AD 602 – and still has much of interest for the visitor. Not quite as far back but certainly going back to the 17th century is the Stirling Arms Hotel which has been host to Bonnie Prince Charlie, the Duke of Argyll and Rabbie Burns who, at one stage, was appointed exciseman in Dunblane. An old coaching inn, full of character and with walls that, no doubt, would have many a good story to tell. It is homely and friendly and welcoming with an extensive menu in the restaurant and good quality inexpensive snacks in the bar or lounge. Probably needs some more money spent on it but its history and its standards make it an interesting and satisfying place to stop.
Proprietors : R L & J Castelow

DUNDEE

THE NO 1
1 Ward Road
Dundee
Tel: 0382 27068

There is quite an impressive appearance to the No 1 situated in the heart of the city and which is a haven for shoppers and businessmen alike. Recently refurbished, the split level lounge offers a high standard of comfort and a pleasant and relaxing ambience. A varied menu is available with 'specials' served daily – both lunchtimes and early evenings – which have earned the pub a well deserved reputation for the quality of food and value for money it offers. Coffee and sandwiches are available from 11 am to 11 pm.
Tennents Taverns

OLD BANK BAR
34 Reform Street
Dundee DD1 1RH
Tel: 0382 26552

A unique pub by virtue of its previous incarnation as a bank. Many of the original features have been retained and used imaginatively in the pub's interior, such as the oak panelling and marble pillars and floors. It is a busy place in the evenings with a predominantly young clientele. Food is available only at lunchtime when there is an extensive and varied menu of freshly prepared food of a good standard. Well worth a visit to experience the unique interior style.
Welcome Inns

THE THREE BARRELS
45 Strathmartine Road
Dundee DD3 7RW
Tel: 0382 810198

A well run city centre pub with a friendly and welcoming atmosphere. Popular with the locals. There is another bar in addition to the lounge bar. Antique wood panelling is a feature. Food is available at lunchtime in the

lounge bar. It is basic pub fare but freshly prepared and generous helpings at reasonable prices. There is a good standard of service from the helpful friendly staff. This 'local' has much to recommend it.
Welcome Inns

DUNFERMLINE

AULD TOLL TAVERN
121 St Leonards Street
Dunfermline, Fife KY11 3AS
Tel: 0383 721489

M90, junction 2. Follow A823 towards town. First licensed premises on left.
A really charming old coaching inn with roots going back a couple of centuries at least. It is quite close to the centre of town with good car parking and a beer garden. Lovely oak beamed interior with good furniture and an excellent atmosphere. There is an extensive menu, reasonably priced. Food is available all day and dinners are served from 5.45 to 10 pm. Service is agreeable and attentive. A well run first class hostelry appealing to all age groups. There are comfortable well fitted bedrooms with colour TV, tea making facilities etc. Children are welcome.
Proprietor: Alan J Ward

THE ELIZABETHAN
Halbeath Road
Dunfermline
KY12 7LX
Tel: 0383 725877

Situated on the busy Halbeath Road that connects with M9 motorway and the centre of the town.
This well-furnished bar in one of Scotland's most historic towns serves morning coffee and food all day from 12 till 9 pm. All meals are home-cooked and two house specials are on the menu each day. Food is of good quality and is very reasonably priced. The staff are efficient and welcoming. The Elizabethan has no delusions of grandeur. It is what it is. A good pub with better than average good value meals. There is a comfortable function room which can be reserved (at no extra charge) for special occasions.
Alloa Brewery

THE HIDEAWAY
Kingseat Road
Halbeath, Dunfermline
Fife KY12 0UB
Tel: 0383 725474

From junction 4 M90, 4 miles. From Forth Bridge, 5 miles.
A charming country pub/restaurant situated on the outskirts of Dunfermline. A courtyard style bar and lounge coupled with a beamed old world restaurant create an attractive ambience and atmosphere all of their own. There is a very extensive range of bar lunches and suppers available every day of the week, and, for the calorie conscious, an extremely extensive salad bar to accompany main courses. The a la carte restaurant has many local dishes such as Loch Fitty trout, grilled in oatmeal and served with locally grown vegetables. The Hideaway prides itself and rightly so on its friendly, professional service and its popularity with local business people and families endorses this.
Proprietor: Ian Kinghorn

PITFIRRANE ARMS HOTEL
Main Street
Crossford
Dunfermline KY12 8NJ
Tel: 0383 736132

On A994 west of Dunfermline.
In by-gone days the Pitfirrane Arms was a coaching inn offering hospitality to olden day travellers stopping there on their arduous journeys about the country. The inn has been carefully restored to retain some of its old world charm and nowadays refreshes a wide variety of people who have not had to endure that bumpy old coach ride! Inside the walls are adorned with pieces of tack and bric-a-brac from the past, giving it old world charm. The bar has a pleasant friendly atmosphere and is frequented by many of the locals. An extremely popular place for good value, good quality bar and restaurant meals.
Proprietor: M McVicars

DYSART

THE ROYAL HOTEL
**Townhead
Dysart
Fife KY1 2XQ
Tel: 0592 52109**

Situated on A955, 2 miles north-east of Kirkcaldy.

This late 18th century coaching inn has earned a high reputation for the excellence of its food and a wide appreciation of the reasonable prices charged. The lounge bar and dining room are furnished with taste, the timber beamed ceilings and the nautical flavour of the decor adding to their attractiveness. There is a wide choice of bar lunches and the dinner menu, very extensive, offers both national and international dishes. The hotel has seven bedrooms with central heating, comfortable modern furniture and each with colour TV. There is a car park to the rear of the hotel and a large function room, recently refurbished, is a popular venue for private functions.
Proprietors: Mr & Mrs I M MacAskill

EAGLESHAM

THE EGLINTON ARMS HOTEL
**Gilmour Street
Eaglesham G76 0LG
Tel: 03553 2631**

Eaglesham is one of Lanarkshire's most charming unspoiled conservation villages. Well worth a visit for its own sake, and just 10 minutes from East Kilbride or 30 minutes from Glasgow city centre. The Eglinton Arms lives up to the attraction of the village. The bars are excellent and very tastefully furnished and there is a good dining room and a function suite. There is very little to find fault with in this place. Food, drink and service are of a high standard and prices very reasonable. All of the bedrooms have an en suite facilities. This must be one of the best pubs in the county and well worth a special journey.
Welcome Inns

SWAN INN
**Polnoon Street
Eaglesham G76 0BH
Tel: 03553 2673**

The Swan is a nice old pub with a character in keeping with Eaglesham's conservation status. The exterior is well maintained and appealing. The atmosphere inside is 'comfortable country' with a mainly local clientele though a lot of the diners are business people or travellers passing through the village. There is an emphasis on straightforward home-cooking and a traditional 'high tea' seems popular. There are real fires in the bar and restaurant areas and the patio windows in the restaurant look out on a well-maintained garden. An excellent range of beers and spirits is available.
Welcome Inns

EAST KILBRIDE

ARCHIES
**Stuart Hotel
2 Cornwall Way
East Kilbride G74 1JR
Tel: 03552 21161**

Located in the centre of the business and shopping area of East Kilbride.

The Stuart Hotel was designed with luxury in mind and the recent refurbishment enhances the aura of stepping into a world of opulence. Archies maintains the standard. It is a very busy place, recognised for its good standard of food and the pleasant staff who provide efficient and speedy service. Meals are served from midday to 9.30 pm and prices are reasonable. The general atmosphere makes you feel welcome. The hotel has 39 bedrooms all with private facilities and furnished to a high standard. Archies is an establishment with much going for it.
Proprietor: Beard Hotels Ltd

LE CAFE

20 Alexandra Way
East Kilbride G74 1LX
Tel: 03552 24177

Just inside East Kilbride's newest shopping mall, immediately adjacent to the car park. East Kilbride's latest eating experience, Le Cafe Bar, has created exactly what this new town has lacked, an inexpensive yet exciting eating place for visitors and locals, be they shoppers, taking a break from the 'High Street', office staff looking for a quick lunchtime snack, or visitors to the area. Hot and cold food is available, starting at 9 am with breakfast, through the morning with coffee and scones baked daily on the premises, to a cold food display over lunch and the afternoon, supplemented by a quality hot bar food menu. Open Monday to Saturday for food; Sunday, bar and light snacks only. East Kilbride has not been too well blessed with interesting places to eat. Le Cafe Bar fills one of the gaps.

Alloa Brewery

EDINBURGH

THE ABBOTSFORD

3 Rose Street
Edinburgh EH2 2PR
Tel: 031 225 5276

Directly behind Jenners, straight up from the Scott Monument.

Situated in the centre of Edinburgh, this delightful public house and restaurant has an old world charm with carved bar counters and pie crust ceilings, tastefully decorated in quiet colours. Enjoying the patronage not only of business people, tourists, shop assistants and their customers and many others, it is also a favourite venue for overseas visitors and has already won an accoloade in the United States as one of the best hostelries in Scotland. Rightly so, as the friendliness of the staff combines easily with a wide range of beers, spirits and wines, second only to the choice and quality of the food, which is served in the bar and restaurant at lunchtime and in the restaurant in the evening. This is a splendid example of a traditional pub. Many hundreds of thousands have beaten a well worn path to its door. You will not be disappointed if you join them.

Proprietor: Colin V Grant

ALBANY HOTEL

39 Albany Street
Edinburgh EH1 3QY
Tel: 031 556 0397

The PM Club Bar of the Albany Hotel has a separate entrance to the lower ground floor, which has been sumptuously transformed into an elegant bar, lounge bar and restaurant. The bar has a predominant library theme but with lots of interesting bric-a-brac and old cameras on display. In an area of the city not over blessed with good bar restaurants the Albany has done well to establish this interesting and attractive bar. The menu is simple but provides an adequate choice of dishes and represents incredibly good value for money. Food is prepared with care and presented with panache and the service is speedy and courteous. Whether for a quick lunch in the bar, a more leisurely meal in the restaurant, or merely a drink with friends, the Club Bar of the Albany makes a very desirable venue.

Proprietor: Mrs P Maridor

THE AULD HOOSE

27-31 William Street
Edinburgh EH3 7NG
Tel: 031 225 5748

Equidistant and parallel to Shandwick Place and Melville Street, west of Princes Street. A pub has to have something to attract and hold its clientele. The Auld Hoose is cosy and quaint, with a very relaxed genuine pub feel about it. It appeals to a complete cross-section of the population. The staff are interested and attentive and make this a pleasant place to drop in for a drink. Some simple straightforward bar snacks.

Alloa Brewery

THE AULD HUNDRED
110-114 Rose Street
Edinburgh EH2 3DT
Tel: 031 225 1809

Rose Street pubs have a quality and character of their own. Each is different from its neighbours, maybe that is why people out to enjoy themselves pop into several of them! The Auld Hundred is at the east end of Edinburgh's pub street. This is very much a traditional pub and is extremely popular with business men, shoppers and tourists all year round. There is a ground floor bar and an upstairs lounge and value for money bar lunches are served from 12 to 2.30 pm (Thursday and Friday 12 to 6 pm).
Alloa Brewery

BARONY BAR
81-85 Broughton Street
Edinburgh EH1 2RJ
Tel: 031 557 0546

The Barony Bar was designed by John Forester in 1898, commissioned by the Trustees of George Sinclair, deceased, wine and spirit merchant. The locality of the bar that was once the ancient Barony Burgh of Broughton – a place notorious as a 'haunt' for witches. The cellars of old Broughton Street once formed the dungeons of the Burgh Tolbooth (demolished 1829) in which followers of the black arts were incarcerated while awaiting execution. The former design of the Barony consisted of Public Bar and Jug and Bar compartment. The well-preserved front of the pub is of teak topped with a huge ornate entablature. One of the many interesting features of the pub is the dado of polychrome tiles which includes tiled pictures of Scottish Scenery. Staff are very pleasant. There is a range of 'different' bar food including vegetarian dishes.
Welcome Inns

BEAU BRUMMELL
99 Hanover Street
Edinburgh EH2 1DJ
Tel: 031 225 4680

Less than 5 minutes walk from Princes Street, in the centre of Edinburgh.
A stylish but traditional lounge bar located in the heart of the city. The Beau Brummell has an attractive blue exterior. The windowed frontage is inviting and the drapes give a touch of elegance. It is a one bar pub with a food counter and salad bar. An extremely comfortable place with tasteful use of brass and chandeliers. The walls are covered with prints. Food is available from 9 am to 3 pm and well into the evening in the summer months. Good value and good quality fare. The service is efficient and the staff diligently attend to keeping the bar area free of the debris of empty glasses etc. This pub has a quality 'feel' about it and attracts a good mix of clientele.
Tennents Taverns

BELLEVUE BAR
49-51 London Street
Edinburgh EH3 6LX
Tel: 031 556 2945

The Bellevue stands boldly on the corner of London Street. It consists of an upstairs lounge where 'live' music can be found on Friday and Saturday evenings. The main attraction of the Bellevue is the downstairs bar. It is a real 'find'. The bar is long and narrow with exposed timber beamed ceiling. There is even a library of old and interesting books, and a domino table. If you cannot find a book of your choice in the library – there is a selection of newspapers available. Exceptionally pleasant and efficient staff. A range of beers and spirits behind a super wooden bar. Toasties, stovies, hot and cold pies and filled rolls are on the menu.
Alloa Brewery
Tenants: Mrs H Salton & Mrs M Strange

BIANCO'S

9 Hope Street
Edinburgh EH2 4EL
Tel: 031 226 2047

When it first opened Bianco's was an interesting new experience on the Edinburgh scene. It still is. Cafe bars of this style and standard are not numerous and this was the original. Converted from a former bank it has the lofty spaciousness that one associates with banks but is yet a pleasantly relaxing meeting place. It opens at 9 am for coffee/tea and croissants etc and continues throughout the day with a changing and appropriate range of light meals. There are good salads from the salad bar at lunchtime as well as speciality filled croissants. Bianco's is licensed all day.
Tennents Taverns

CAFE ÇA VA

133 High Street
Edinburgh EH1 1SG
Tel: 031 556 3276

On the 'Royal Mile' close to North Bridge. One of a new range of cafe style pubs which opened in Edinburgh a few years ago. Re-decorated in 1989, this brasserie offers a comfortable and relaxing atmosphere away from the busy shopping area and yet in the heart of the historic Royal Mile. Cafe Ca Va is licensed all day and there is a wide range of both hot and cold lunches served daily. Try the charcoal grilled specialities which are particularly popular. A well managed pub with high standards and a sound reputation with its clientele, drawn from both local residents and tourists.
Tennents Taverns

CAFE ST JAMES

25 St James Centre
Edinburgh EH1 3SS
Tel: 031 557 2631

Cafe St James is a cafe bar situated on the roof of the St James Centre at the east end of Princes Street, and has built up an excellent reputation for good bar food. A cafe bar is not the easiest of places to which to give an identity and character of its own but it comes off well here. The pleasant interior with lots of tables and lots of small curtained windows has quite a cafe feel about it at lunchtime. A very good standard obtained here, a reflection on good management. On Thursday, Friday and Saturday evenings it features over 25s disco nights when a good time is had by all.
Alloa Brewery

CAMBRIDGE BAR

20 Young Street
Edinburgh EH2 4JB
Tel: 031 225 4266

Much less brash than Rose Street, this is a much quieter and more restrained area to the north of George Street with one or two pleasant pubs. The Cambridge is one of these. Our inspector was quite taken with it and found the atmosphere congenial and comfortable with a friendly clientele. A polite and welcoming barmaid made her customers feel at home. A blackboard menu lists quite an extensive range of bar meals. The Cambridge does not pretend to be the cocktail bar of a grand hotel nor does it go to the other extreme. It is a good class warm attractive pub and a very enjoyable place in which to spend an hour or two.
Alloa Brewery
Tenant: Mr & Mrs Tony John

CROWN & CUSHION

Jocks Lodge
Edinburgh
Tel: 031 661 1800

The Crown & Cushion is conveniently situated near to Meadowbank Stadium at Jocks Lodge junction. There is attractive alcove seating which is always popular when you want to have a degree of privacy, yet doesn't exclude the wider atmosphere of the pub. Food is not pretentious but is carefully tailored to the market it serves and is of good quality and very moderate in price. Bar lunches are served at normal lunchtimes Monday to Saturday and the service is friendly and helpful. This pub gives the impression of being well managed, of knowing its customers, and looking after them. There is a nice intimate feel to it and it

will be a good establishment for locals and office workers from the large office development nearby.
Alloa Brewery
Tenant: Bob Nimmo

DEACON BRODIES
435 Lawnmarket
Edinburgh EH1 2NT
Tel: 031 225 6531

Deacon Brodies occupies a prime position at the top of the Mound in the High Street, Edinburgh. It is ideally situated close to the Law Courts, City Chambers, Edinburgh University and numerous tourist attractions such as St Giles Cathedral and Edinburgh Castle. The tavern is named after one of Edinburgh's more infamous residents, William Brodie, and it was Brodie's baseness that inspired Robert Louis Stevenson to write the famous classic – Dr Jekyll and Mr Hyde. Look out for scenes of robbery and Brodie's execution which are depicted in murals on the walls of the tavern. Excellent bar meals are served at lunchtime and throughout most of the evening in both bars where you can sit and enjoy views of St Giles Cathedral and King George IV Bridge. Coffee and tea available every day from 10 am. A splendid old pub, steeped in history.
Alloa Brewery

THE DOCTORS
32 Forrest Road
Edinburgh EH1 2QN
Tel: 031 225 1819

The Doctors, close to Greyfriars Bobby and the University prescribes the best in cask ales, wines and spirits, and less potent low alcohol 'medicine'. To take your mind off your troubles there is a fascinating array of apothecary jars from bygone days. The interior alcove-style seating is of leather and wood, much of it retained and restored from the original premises. This is not a pretentious pub but it is well located to draw in medical students from the University (hence its name) and visitors to the nearby Royal Infirmary. Bar lunches are available at reasonable prices from 12 to 2.30pm. The pub stays open till 1 am at weekends for late night socialisers.
Welcome Inns

ENSIGN EWART
521 Lawnmarket
Edinburgh EH1 2PE
Tel: 031 225 7440

Historic pub at the start of the Royal Mile in the shadow of Edinburgh Castle. There has been a pub on this site for more than 300 years. Originally known as the Hole in the Wall the name was changed in celebration of Ensign Ewart's heroic action at the Battle of Waterloo. The daily lunch menu features traditional cooking, is inexpensive and seems to appeal to the mainly tourist clientele. A lively atmosphere in the evenings when the Ensign Ewart becomes the gathering place for fans of folk music. This is the first pub on the way down the Royal Mile from the Castle and a good place to fortify oneself before the mile long trek to Holyrood.
Alloa Brewery
Tenant: Bryan McCann

THE FAIRMILE INN
42 Biggar Road
Edinburgh EH10 7BJ
Tel: 031 445 2056

A large whitewashed roadhouse surrounded by car parks on a busy arterial route and close to the city bypass. It has commanding views of the Pentland Hills and the Moorfoot Hills beyond. There is a nice airy open feel about the interior as rooms merge into one another. The lounge area is on a raised level with attractive bamboo furnishings. Bar food is available all day, and the restaurant has value for money table d'hote menus of good standard and modest prices. A lot of careful effort has gone into transforming what was once an undistinguished roadhouse into the attractive pub it is today.
Welcome Inns

THE FAMOUS PEACOCK INN

The Harbour
Newhaven
Edinburgh EH6 4HZ
Tel: 031 552 5522/8707

By taxi from Princes Street, 10 minutes. Bus Nos. 16, 22, 10, 9, 11, 7 pass the door.
The Peacock is a very famous old hostelry going back well over 200 years, known to generations of Edinburghers as well as its own faithful 'locals'. Newhaven itself is steeped in history and the Peacock reflects much of it. The Free Fishermen of Newhaven is one of the oldest guild societies in the country and the present proprietor of the Peacock, Peter Carnie, and his son are both members of this 400 year old Society. The food is neither fancy nor pretentious but it is good quality well prepared fare in generous portions and at very inexpensive prices. There is something for every age group in this distinguished old inn, full of character and interest.
Proprietor: Peter Carnie

GARRICK BAR

7 Spittal Street
Edinburgh EH3 9DY
Tel: 031 229 8368

Close to junction of Spittal Street and Bread Street and near cinema complex in Lothian Road.
The busy and friendly Garrick Bar is a convenient venue for a break for visitors and shoppers alike with Lothian Road, the Grassmarket, the Royal Mile and the Castle all within a few minutes walking distance. There is an excellent pub food menu, varied, interesting and good value with a wide choice of dishes all day. In this city centre area this is a pub that has concentrated on the quality of food to attract and hold its clientele. There is a good range of beers and lagers but if your choice is something stronger be warned, spirits here are served in the larger but traditional, ¼ gill measure.
Alloa Brewery
Tenant: Campbell Main

THE GOLD MEDAL TAVERN

58 Dalkeith Road
Edinburgh EH14 1TG
Tel: 031 667 1816

The Gold Medal, which took this name following a refurbishment at one time when the Commonwealth Games were held in Edinburgh, is situated on the Dalkeith Road, opposite Edinburgh's Commonwealth Swimming Pool, and in close proximity to the city's famous landmarks, Holyrood Palace, the Royal Mile and Arthur's Seat. It is a large attractive detached building with plenty of car parking and, in summer, a spacious out-of-doors area for those who want to contemplate Arthur's Seat while sipping their ale. There is a lounge bar and public bar serving food all day and a restaurant called Waffles offering an interesting and varied menu with emphasis on home-cooking. Coach parties and function parties of up to 100 persons are catered for.
Alloa Brewery

GREYFRIARS BOBBY

34 Candlemaker Row
Edinburgh EH1 2QE
Tel: 031 225 8300

One of Edinburgh's favourite tourist attractions is the Greyfriars Churchyard where the world's best known dog kept watch over the grave of his master, John Gray, from 1856 to 1872. The memory of Bobby is kept alive by the books and the Walt Disney film telling Bobby's story. The pub Greyfriars Bobby is situated on the grounds of the Churchyard and over the years has developed an excellent reputation for a varied menu serving quality meals at reasonable prices. Meals are served from 12 to 9 pm. Various souvenirs of Bobby himself can also be purchased. A good pub for both tourists and locals alike.
Alloa Brewery

GROSVENOR BAR

28 Shandwick Place
Edinburgh EH2 4RT
Tel: 031 226 4579

Originally opened in 1890, the Grosvenor recently underwent a transformation for its hundreth year. Many original features are retained and nowadays the French-style cafe doors opening on to the street, give an airy cosmopolitan feel to this fashionable West End cafe bar. The restored bar gantry features cask ales, malt whiskies, and less potent low alcohol products. There is an interestingly displayed menu with lunchtime food ranging from baked potatoes to steak sandwiches. Coffee and patiseries are served from 10 am till close – which at weekends is 1 am! Service is friendly and efficient. Although the clientele embraces all age groups it is predominantly a pub for younger people and as such it is lively and popular.
Welcome Inns

HARRY'S BAR

7B Randolph Place
Edinburgh EH3 7TE
Tel: 031 226 2979

Less than five minutes from the West End of Princes Street.
Harry's is a basement bar and restaurant minutes from Edinburgh's West End. It is popular with business people in the area as a rendezvous for lunch and drinks after work. The entrance may be unimpressive but once inside the atmosphere is that of an 'in' place to be! The long bar is the first thing you see as you come down the final couple of steps inside. Blue tiffany style lamps add a touch of elegance and colour to the bar area, which opens up to a dining area. The large windows – so rare in basement premises – give another dimension to the room. Food is served at lunchtime only and is of a very good standard – not your run of the mill but range from crepes to steak sandwiches, all very well presented. An interesting collection of pub memorabilia on the walls makes this place that bit different.
Proprietors: The West Brothers

THE HAYMARKET

11-14 West Maitland Street
Edinburgh EH9 1TF
Tel: 031 229 5647

The Haymarket dominates the road intersection on which it stands. It has an attractive external appearance in black and gold and curves round the shape of the building of which it is part. Inside there is a good use of stained glass, nice intimate alcoves and an excellent overall atmosphere. Food is available all day and is of good standard with lunches being particularly popular and remarkable value. The public areas are clearly well maintained and well supervised. We used a local businessman to assess this pub and he finished his report by saying "This is one of my favourite pubs of those visited. Good beer, clean interesting environment. Bliss!"
Alloa Brewery

THE HUNTER'S TRYST

97 Oxgangs Road
Edinburgh EH13 9NG
Tel: 031 445 3132

The Hunter's Tryst is situated overlooking the Pentland Hills and Edinburgh's famous all year round ski facility. In the 18th and 19th centuries the Tryst was a popular meeting place for hunters and was renowned for the excellence of its fare. Today, the Hunter's Tryst offers equally high standards and is a particularly suitable meeting place for families and business people alike. Lunch and Sunday brunch are a feature at the Tryst. A good up-market local pub meeting the demands of this largely residential district, but also a place to which people drive from quite far afield.
Alloa Brewery

THE KENILWORTH

152-154 Rose Street
Edinburgh EH2 3JD
Tel: 031 225 8100

One of the famous pubs in this famous street. A very attractive end of terrace pub with lots of hanging baskets and traditional appearance. The Kenilworth was once a butcher's shop and still retains the beautiful

tiled walls. The centre isle bar with its interestingly carved gantry dispenses a range of cask conditioned beers together with good wholesome food served during all opening hours. Good old fashioned hospitality is the order of the day at the Kenilworth. Lots of oak, a superb red and white painted ceiling, nice stained glass windows and two lovely brass chandeliers make this an immensely appealing pub. For true traditional pub atmosphere this really is a must.
Alloa Brewery

KINLEITH ARMS
**604 Lanark Road
Juniper Green
Edinburgh EH14 5EN
Tel: 031 453 3214**

In the evening with its floodlights on this bright whitewashed building with car park it looks very attractive and welcoming. It has a central 'V' shaped bar serving a number of open plan areas and the overall ambience is very pleasant and relaxed. You can have morning coffee from opening time and bar lunches from 12 to 2 pm. Prices are reasonable, quality is good. Service is of a very high standard and seems to stay that way no matter how busy the pub becomes. This is predominantly a 'local' and a good one, but visitors would feel very much at home and be made welcome.
Alloa Brewery

THE LAST DROP
**74-78 Grassmarket
Edinburgh EH1 2JR
Tel: 031 225 4851**

As well as being a main city market place Edinburgh's Grassmarket was the site of the public gallows. The Last Drop is so called to commemorate the last public hanging in the Grassmarket. The pub is only a few steps away from the very site on which the original gallows stood, and has the distinction of being the only building in the Grassmarket to have retained its original form and design from the outside. Obviously a pub of historical interest, which many will wish to visit, and where not only can you sample the atmosphere of Edinburgh's old town but also enjoy a relaxing drink and quality bar lunches served in a unique surrounding.
Alloa Brewery

LIBERTON INN
**89-90 Kirk Brae
Liberton
Edinburgh EH16 6JA
Tel: 031 664 3102**

This traditional and bustling pub is situated next to the church in old Liberton. It is attractively decorated in green with hanging flower baskets. Parking is not too easy at times. The bars and restaurant have feature fireplaces which add to the old style character of the inn. There is a pleasing clean feel to the lounge area which is comfortable and well decorated. Reuben Butler's Pantry is named after the husband of Jeannie Deans who was the central figure in Sir Walter Scott's novel 'The Heart of Midlothian', and who is reputed to have lived in the premises adjoining the room. The extensive bar menu is available from 12 to 2 pm and 7 to 11 pm, and children are welcome. This is a good local pub with high standards throughout and as one would expect in any good local it has a comfortable mix of age groups.
Tennents Taverns

THE MAGNUM
1 Albany Street
Edinburgh EH1 3PY
Tel: 031 557 4366

The Magnum is an extremely popular up-market wine bar and restaurant which has earned a deservedly high reputation. It is well located just a few hundred yards from the business centre of St Andrew Square, the bus station and Waverley Railway Station. It has recently been renovated with care and taste. It is elegant without being overbearing and the layout is such that it is also cosy and intimate. The Wine Bar is very much an 'in' meeting place for a pleasant drink with friends or an aperitif before eating. The dining room offers serious food presented with panache. This is a well planned, well managed establishment of high standard.

THE MAYBURY
Maybury Road
Edinburgh EH12
Tel: 031 339 1430

Roadhouses were perhaps a phenomenon of the 1930s and were usually located on the outskirts of towns and cities. The Maybury is a splendid example. Constructed to look like a ship, it has carefully been restored to its former elegance in magnificent art deco style. The entrance lounge bar is spacious and stylish, and here you can enjoy a reasonable range of light bar meals. For those with more time on their hands, there is an open mezzanine floor overlooking the bar where more substantial meals are available from a sophisticated menu. There are also private meeting rooms and a function suite. All in all this is a first class example of a restored art deco establishment of substance and style.
Welcome Inns

THE MERLIN
168 Morningside Road
Edinburgh EH10 4PU
Tel: 031 447 4329

A large two storey building set back from the busy road. It has an attractive glass frontage which can be opened giving a cafe effect. The premises have recently been modernised featuring a lot of wood and an attractive raised island bar. In this open spacious area there is plenty of seating and a restaurant in one corner. The Merlin is open all day for food from 10 am and has a good medium priced menu. The service is good and efficient, which it has to be in such a busy and popular rendezvous as this. A good all-round modern pub attracting a wide range of ages and a good clientele.
Welcome Inns

MINDERS BAR
112-114 Causewayside
Edinburgh
Tel: 031 667 9479

Attractive though small ground floor of a two storey terraced building on a busy thoroughfare, Minders is very well and comfortably furnished making the most of the relatively small bar/lounge space. It is a good meeting and socialising point for local business people, residents and students. There is a limited bar snack menu, probably due to lack of kitchen space, but what there is seems good value. The atmosphere created by the size of the place and comfortable furnishings makes this an enjoyable and lively pub to visit.
Proprietor: Mrs A S Thomson

THE MURRAYFIELD HOTEL
18 Corstorphine Road
Edinburgh EH12 6HN
Tel: 031 337 1844

On Corstorphine Road on the way into Edinburgh city from the west, immediately adjacent to Murrayfield rugby ground. The Murrayfield must be known to hundreds of thousands of rugby fans over the decades and is very much 'the' popular before and after match rendezvous. Excellent value food of high quality served in pleasant surroundings in this fine old hotel in Scotland's capital city. The restaurant is open for dinner seven nights and any lunchtime by arrangement, but good value interesting bar snacks add an

additional element to the established catering base. Just a little out from the west end of the city centre the Murrayfield has earned its own special niche in the life of the city and its millions of visitors. The 23 bedrooms have recently been refurbished to a high standard and all have private facilities.
Alloa Brewery

NAVAAR HOUSE HOTEL
12 Mayfield Gardens
Edinburgh EH9 2BZ
Tel: 031 667 2828

This is a Victorian building with many fine features. It has six letting bedrooms all with tea/coffee making facilities and colour TV. Five rooms have showers. From summer 1990, all rooms will have en suite facilities. There are two traditional bars selling excellent real ales and guest beers. Home-cooked bar meals are served seven days. Lunches 12 to 2.30 pm and evening meals 6.30 to 8.30 pm. Every Tuesday evening you can enjoy the sounds of the Louisianna Ragtime Jazz Band. Why not drop in and enjoy it!
Proprietor : Mrs A S Thomson

P J CLARKE'S NEW YORK CAFE
80 Queen Street
Edinburgh EH4 2NF
Tel: 031 220 2052

A fairly recent addition to the Edinburgh scene is P J Clarke's. In the style of a New York bar, it has a spacious and open feel to it. Bare floor boards, small wooden tables and wicker chairs give it an American saloon atmosphere. There is a large mural of a New York scene stretching from the ground floor to the basement diner – quite a feature! At lunchtime there is a good salad bar at the end of the long bar counter, and food ranges from filled croissants to steaks and baked potatoes. The best atmosphere is when the place is really busy, but that is most of the time as it is a popular meeting place for young business people.
Proprietor: T Finlay

PADDY'S BAR
49 Rose Street
Edinburgh EH2 2NH
Tel: 031 225 6362

Rose Street, of course, is famous for its pubs and Paddy's is well-known to anyone who has ever passed along this street. It is a one-room traditional pub with a food counter. Lots of wood and bric-a-brac and tasteful use of brass. Gingham tablecloths at lunchtime and flowers on the tables. Food is simple but of good quality and the staff are efficient and friendly. This is a pleasant pub usually bustling and busy and one that most people feel comfortable in. It has some fun party nights.
Alloa Brewery

PENGUIN CAFE
26 Frederick Street
Edinburgh EH2 2JR
Tel: 031 225 4285

This well situated city centre site has been delightfully transformed in bar brasserie style and is now an excellent rendezvous with a comfortable relaxed air to it. It is really in three sections – the restaurant with a polished parquet floor and coloured prints crowding the walls; the bar with a combination of low tables and chairs and high stool seating, plus a boothed seating area. A fairly wide range of good food is available in the bar till about 6 pm and a much wider menu in the brasserie restaurant, all of high standard. There is no doubt that a lot of thought and care has gone into the planning of this establishment and the effort has not been wasted. Although this may be seen as aimed primarily at the younger set it will appeal to all age groups, and increasingly will make its mark on the Edinburgh scene.
Proprietor: Stakis plc

THE PUB
119 Rose Street
Edinburgh EH2 3DT
Tel: 031 225 3982

This is a really smart and modern pub in the heart of Rose Street Precinct and is very different in style and character to some of its more traditional neighbours. It was the city's original disco pub and has a strong following. However, 'The Pub' transforms itself over the lunchtime period to accommodate shoppers, businessmen and tourists alike with quality traditional food. Immaculate decor and quality lighting make this a very good theme pub. Sound management and interested staff contribute to making this a high quality pub.
Alloa Brewery

QUEEN'S ARMS
47-49 Frederick Street
Edinburgh EH2 1EP
Tel: 031 225 1045

A splendidly fitted out downstairs bar in the city centre. Dark wood beams, dark panelling, horse brasses and bric-a-brac combine to recreate an atmosphere which is elsewhere slipping away from us in starkly modern premises. A compact busy bar at front leads into a very spacious lounge with comfortable seats and beaten copper-topped tables. The serving staff are helpful and speedy and crisply turned out. There is a reasonable range of popular dishes. This is a pub that is nearly always busy – and rightly so. It has something!
Alloa Brewery
Tenant: Terry Doherty

THE RAEBURN
2-4 Raeburn Place
Edinburgh EH4 1HN
Tel: 031 332 6345

North of Princes Street, 1 mile. Stockbridge contains some of the finest architecture in Edinburgh's New Town and is extremely popular with tourists who visit the many antique shops for a piece of Edinburgh's history or walk along the newly developed walkway by the 'Water of Leith'. The Raeburn Bar, at the corner of Raeburn Place in Stockbridge, was refurbished in 1987. It offers an excellent range of quality snacks at a reasonable price and is an ideal stopping place before or after browsing round Stockbridge. It gives evidence of a well-managed establishment really interested in looking after its customers.
Alloa Brewery

ROSE STREET BREWERY
55-59 Rose Street
Edinburgh EH2 2NR
Tel: 031 220 1227

Amongst the many famous and popular public houses in Edinburgh's Rose Street, the Rose Street Brewery must rank as special. It is certainly the most unique. Indeed, it is the only mainland 'brew pub' in Scotland. The two beers brewed on the premises are Auld Reekie 80/- and 90/- and visits to the brewery can be arranged most days of the year. A beer lover's paradise. The Rose Street Brewery also provides customers with an excellent menu which is available from midday through to 9 pm. Included in this is their 'Bullocks Steakhouse' which features from 5 pm. There is an air of showplace originality about this establishment. It set out to be different and it is.
Alloa Brewery

THE ROYAL ARCHER
1 Jeffrey Street/
1 High Street
Edinburgh EH1 1SR
Tel: 031 556 6338

One of the good pubs on the Royal Mile between Edinburgh Castle and the Palace of Holyroodhouse. It stands on the corner of the High Street and Jeffrey Street, has recently been refurbished and externally looks very attractive. There is a small intimate lounge bar of pleasing decor and a bright well finished central bar area with seating around the walls. A good basic menu is available all day at average prices. The

premises are kept in good condition and though this is an old building it has a clean bright feel to it. The mixed clientele - a mixture of tourists, local office staff, casual visitors etc adds to the flavour of the place. A welcoming pub – both inside and out.
Alloa Brewery

THE ROYAL MILE TAVERN
**127 High Street
Edinburgh EH1
Tel: 031 556 8274**

The Royal Mile from Edinburgh Castle to Holyroodhouse has nearly as many good pubs as has Rose Street. This is one of them. Situated on the High Street between Bishops Close and North Greys Close, the attractive external appearance of the appropriately named Royal Mile Tavern invites you in to an equally pleasing interior. The bar lounge is long and narrow and perhaps its smallness is a contributing factor in creating an intimate and friendly ambience. A good range of food is available, from morning coffee at 9 to 11 am through lunches till 3 pm and dinners from 6 to 9 pm. A speciality to try is fresh mussels in wine with garlic sauce. This is a neat and tidy pub of good traditional standard, though thoroughly up to date and likely to appeal to locals and visitors alike.
Tenant: Frank S Mickel

RUTLAND HOTEL
**3 Rutland Street
Edinburgh EH1 2AA
Tel: 031 229 3402/3**

Next to the Caledonian Hotel at the west end of Princes Street.
The award winning premises in Edinburgh's West End with a superb view along Princes Street. The ground floor bar, No 1 Rutland Place, is one of the liveliest evening venues in the city and an equally convenient and popular meeting place for coffee, lunch or a sandwich at any other time of day. L'Attache, the basement wine bar, is a must for lovers of authentic stone vaults, candlelit tables and excellent healthy food. In the evenings it is a popular folk venue with live music five nights a week. The first floor Gallery and Restaurant offers a more relaxed atmosphere and a very reasonably priced menu, together with an unusual balcony overlooking the ground floor No 1 Bar. There are 17 letting bedrooms, most with private facilities. The Rutland would rank high in any list of the top 10 pubs in the city. Its site alone would ensure popularity but everything about this place seems right.
Welcome Inns

SCOTTS
**202 Rose Street
Edinburgh EH2 4AZ
Tel: 031 225 7401**

Scott's bar has been going strongly since 1844 and shows no sign of ever running out of appeal. It has recently been refurbished, but this has been done sympathetically and it has lost none of the traditional character that has made it one of the best known and most popular bars in the west end of Rose Street. Get along early if you wish to sample the bar's traditional fare served from 12 noon. It is home-made, tasty and remarkably modest in price. Scott's popularity ensures that it is nearly always busy, but this one-room pub has that kind of attraction.
Alloa Brewery

SHEEP HEID INN
**43 The Causeway
Duddingston
Edinburgh EH15 3QA
Tel: 031 661 1020**

The Sheep Heid Inn is one of the oldest licensed premises in Scotland, and has always been renowned for its traditional cooking and friendly service, while its unique recreational activity, skittles, is said to attract people from all over Scotland at some time. It is situated in the main street of the historic village of Duddingston. Internally it has been superbly laid out with a good island bar and a comfortable intimate atmosphere. There is a beer garden for the long summer evenings and quite frequently a barbecue in operation. The restaurant prides itself on its special Scottish dishes, concentrating on the best of fresh local produce. This is a pub that is very hard to fault. Lots of Edinburgh's many tourists find their way to it and like the locals would commend it as an excellent pub in every aspect.

Tennents Taverns

STARBANK INN & RESTAURANT

**64 Laverockbank Road
Edinburgh EH5 3BZ
Tel: 031 552 4141**

This is a well-maintained building in a very charming part of Edinburgh. The lounge is spacious and 'L' shaped with a enviable selection of antique beer trays decorating the walls and water jugs hooked on the beamed ceiling. The menu is extensive and reasonable. Bar lunches Monday to Saturday 12 to 2.30 pm. Sunday family lunch 12.30 to 3 pm (at bar 4pm). Meals Tuesday to Sunday 6.45 to 10 pm (Sunday 5 to 8 pm) 'eaterie' or lounge. Charming and efficient bar staff with the attitude that the 'customer always comes first!' Nine real ales to tempt you. The Starbank exudes an atmosphere that makes you feel that you are on holiday, the clientele contributes to this feeling. Don't be put off by the cold sea air as there are cosy open fires to keep you warm in the winter. Families welcome.

Belhaven Brewery

THE TATTLER

**23 Commercial Street
Edinburgh EH6 6JA
Tel: 031-554 9999**

In Leith Port area where the Water of Leith joins the docks.
The renovation of Leith has done much more than clean up the exterior of some of its fine buildings. It has breathed new life into the place and brought to public attention a number of fine up-market bars and restaurants. The Tattler is a typical example. Very nicely styled and furnished with a warm and cosy atmosphere. It has an excellent range of really good bar meals and its main restaurant is a member of the prestigious Taste of Scotland Scheme.

With a level of service to match the quality of the food, this is very much a pub restaurant of the very best type with a price range to suit all income levels and a standard better than most.

Proprietor: Thomson Taverns

THE THREE TUNS

**7-11 Hanover Street
Edinburgh EH2 2DL
Tel: 031 225 5412**

The Three Tuns is just off the centre point of Edinburgh's famous Princes Street. It is a basement bar with a great deal of atmosphere and character offering its clientele an excellent salad bar available all day. Food is of high standard and so is the staff. The Three Tuns has an interesting and varied wine list and offers a selection of unusual Scottish wines e.g. raspberry, silver birch, blackberry and elderflower. A credit to its owners and management.

Alloa Brewery

THE TRADING POST

**31-34 The Shore
Leith
Edinburgh EH6 6QN
Tel: 031 553 5153**

The old port of Leith has seen many changes over the past decade but none more dramatic perhaps than the improvements along this most interesting stretch of the waterfront – now very much an 'in' place for a leisurely evening out. The Trading Post is quite an experience. American in overall concept with a touch of the old corral. It is a 'cook-your-own' set up with fixed barbecue grills on each table and a wide range of salads and desserts at a counter. The staff are attentive and helpful. This is a place that is very different. It will appeal particularly to the young but everyone would enjoy the different atmosphere and the novelty of cooking your own grill. Starting off with good quality raw materials you cannot go too far wrong. A place for an enjoyable meal experience.

Proprietor: The McFarlane Group

VICTORIA & ALBERT

15-17 Frederick Street
Edinburgh EH2 2EY

Tel: 031 226 4562

The Victoria and Albert is situated in the heart of Edinburgh's New Town. It was opened with a full Victorian pageant on 21 October 1968. Before that, the building had been a licensed grocer's and dated back to the 18th century. The Victoria and Albert tries to combine the best of Victorian conviviality, food is available all day and the evening is the time to sing-along with the honky-tonk piano and enjoy the good selection of dishes available on the a la carte menu. A most comfortable pub with lots of character, with appeal for every age group.
Alloa Brewery

THE WATERFRONT WINE BAR

1c Dock Place
Leith
Edinburgh
EH6 6LU
Tel: 031 554 7427

Right on the waterfront at Leith, this very popular establishment has been converted from a dockside waiting room with an added conservatory and outside tables fronting the water. It is a convivial bistro style bar, a place where people go for an informal evening out in an interesting friendly atmosphere rather than just dropping in for a drink. There is an unusual and varied menu of starters, main dishes and desserts, and of better standard than many similar establishments. The Waterfront is already a firm favourite with a large section of the Edinburgh public and is increasingly sought out by visitors to the city. It has a lot going for it and is well worth a visit.
Proprietors: Messrs Bowie, Reid & Ruthven

WHIGHAMS WINE CELLARS

13 Hope Street
Edinburgh EH2
Tel: 031 225 9717

In the vaults of the rather stately building fringing on Charlotte Square, Whighams is a lively wine bar within the character of this centuries old location. There are stone walls, original flagstones and sawdust on the floor! Hooks and wires hang from the ceiling and an old map of Portugal on the wall showing different wine areas. Altogether a very unique atmosphere has been created - seating is available in various areas of the low ceilinged vaults. There are excellent and unusual items on the menu including smoked venison and oysters in season. There is a wonderful range of wines to tempt all connoisseurs of the grape.

THE WINE GLASS

1 Newington Road
Edinburgh EH9 1QR
Tel: 031 667 6868

The Wine Glass in Newington is a well-known landmark in the Edinburgh scene. It has a good welcoming feel to it and recent re-decoration has enhanced the interior appeal. This is a particularly popular lunchtime rendezvous and the atmosphere is usually convivial. Varied and good value meals are available at lunchtime except Sundays and may range from quick snacks to speciality steaks. There are usually fresh flowers on the tables. The Wine Glass appeals to a wide age group. It is on the fringe of the city centre on a main arterial route and close to university halls of residence. Its standards make it a good meeting and socialising point.
Tennents Taverns
Tenant : Alan Robertson

WORLD'S END PUB & RESTAURANT

2-8 The High Street
Edinburgh
EH1 1TB
Tel: 031 556 3628

Standing in the Royal Mile on the corner of St Mary's Street, the World's End is so named as it lies on the boundary site of the old city wall of Edinburgh. Inside there is a genuine welcome and an ambience of old world charm. This is a pub which is conveniently placed for tourists drifting down the Royal Mile but also caters for locals and has its regular clientele. Among the beers on sale is a good range of Belhaven conditioned ales, which are still brewed at the old brewery at Dunbar, East Lothian. There is a reasonable range of inexpensive bar food to enjoy before continuing to explore the other charms of the City of Edinburgh.

Belhaven Brewery
Tenant : D Miller

YE OLD GOLF TAVERN

30 Wrights Houses
Bruntsfield
Edinburgh EH10 4HR
Tel: 031 229 3235

Established in 1456 and reputedly the oldest pub in central Edinburgh. The Golf Tavern overlooks Bruntsfield Links where King James III is said to have practised his swing prior to frequenting the tavern. This is an exceptional pub with good bar layout, good service and attractive seating with leather Chesterfield settees. Its closeness to the nearby King's Theatre makes it popular as a rendezvous before or after a show. Starting with coffee and croissants at 10 am, the Golf offers an interesting range of hot and cold food throughout the day, with an emphasis on vegetarian and healthy eating. Staff are very helpful and efficient. The upper rooms will shortly be available for small functions, buffets and meetings. For ambience, comfort, good beer and food this ranks very high amongst the city's pubs.

Welcome Inns

YE OLDE INN

25 Main Street
Davidsons Mains
Edinburgh
EH4 5BZ
Tel: 031 336 2437

Ye Olde Inn, Davidsons Mains, is a quaint old pub offering an excellent selection of ales in its two bars. Tasty home-made bar lunches and suppers are served every day. A cottage style pub in this virtually unchanged village suburb. Leaded windows and hanging baskets of flowers add to its charm, and there is usually a welcoming coal fire in the lounge. Lots of beams and dark stained wood in the interior. Ye Olde Inn is a typical local meeting the needs of local area residents, business people and shoppers. It has an excellent selection of ales in its two bars. Tasty snacks and bar lunches and suppers are served daily. The inn's new conservatory is a particularly attractive feature together with the extensive beer garden at the back which proves to be a very popular meeting place in the balmy summer evenings. A pub with a nice comfortable village feel to it.

Alloa Brewery

ELGIN

THE ABBEY COURT RESTAURANT

15 Greyfriars Street
Elgin
Moray
IV30 1LF
Tel: 0343 542849

Central Elgin behind Council Buildings. This is really a bar restaurant with strong emphasis on food, and comfortable and relaxed surroundings. The Abbey Court offers its customers the full range of services – morning coffee, bar and business lunch, a la carte lunch, afternoon coffee and snacks and a la carte dinners. The menu is extensive featuring much of the fresh produce available locally – fresh fish and seafood, Scotch beef and lamb, Spey salmon, venison, hare, pheasant and partridge. Additionally, a selection of continental dishes and a full range of home-made pasta are available. Do not be put off by the unimpressive external appearance which does not do justice to the operation within. This is a first class establishment of high standard with a warm friendly atmosphere and value for money. Closed Sunday.

Proprietors : B A Chown & C M Pitstra

CLOUSEAU'S

**48a High Street
Elgin
IV30 1BY
Tel: 0343 549737**

Off High Street (up Red Lion Close). Located in one of Elgin's noted closes, in a very historic part of the city, this 18th century mill warehouse was tastefully converted to its present use in 1985. Presented with the Bronze Award in the Wine Bar of the Year 1989. The wine list is diverse and interesting with 12 bins available by the glass. A wide range of beers and spirits is also offered. The bar menu offers a wide variety, catering for all tastes both at lunchtime and in the evening. The upper floor restaurant is open every evening for those looking for a more formal setting. While the primary appeal may be to the younger generation there is something here for all types and all age groups.

Proprietor : Elizabeth M Wilson

THE DIP INN

**Mansion House Hotel
The Haven
Elgin
IV30 1AW
Tel: 0343 548811**

Behind Elgin's tallest monument. The Mansion House is a fine up-market hotel with an excellent reputation, and the 'Dip Inn' is a special feature of it. It overlooks the hotel's magnificent swimming pool and exudes an atmosphere of relaxation and luxury. There is a wide variety of snacks and grills available all day from 11 am till about 11 pm yet the menu is remarkably inexpensive considering the surroundings and facilities. A very attractive place from every aspect. The Mansion House Hotel and Country Club is a member of the prestigious Tast of Scotland Scheme and it goes without saying that the restaurant is very highly commended for those wishing more formal eating or a wider choice. The hotel has some superb accommodation. Altogether a very highly rated establishment.

Proprietor : Fernando Oliveira

THUNDERTON HOUSE

**Thunderton Lane
Elgin
IV30 1BG
Tel: 0343 548767**

Thunderton Inn, situated in the centre of the town is a traditional pub in every sense of the word. It is reputed that Bonnie Prince Charlie stayed at the Thunderton before the Battle of Culloden. The extensive and imaginative menu is served all day in both the bar and lounge and is well complemented by the fine selection of Scottish and English traditional ales served from hand pumps. The family room welcomes children all day, so everyone can experience the charm of old Scotland that is the Thunderton Inn.

Tennents Taverns

ELLON

THE BUCHAN HOTEL

**1 Bridge Street
Ellon
Aberdeenshire
AB4 9AA
Tel: 0358 20208**

On A94, Peterhead-Fraserburgh road, 14 miles from Aberdeen, turn left at the roundabout ending dual carriageway on to Ellon. The hotel sits on the bridge end.

An impressive building in the city centre overlooking the River Ythan. It has been totally refurbished recently to a very high standard. The Buchan has a good reputation for its food and specialises in the wide variety of game which is so plentiful in that area. There is a strong emphasis on honest home-cooking. Bread is baked on the premises and home-made sweets feature in

the desserts. Standards in this establishment are excellent. It is well-appointed and busy - and deserves to be. The proprietors are very much involved in the daily operation of the hotel and their presence sets the tone. There are 17 bedrooms all with private bathrooms and the usual facilities.
Proprietors: Robert & Rosaline Kelman

EYEMOUTH

THE CRAW INN
**Auchencrow, Nr Reston
Eyemouth
Berwickshire
TD14 5LS
Tel: 08907 61253**

Off A1 at Houndwood on B6437 Chirnside road – second left then first right (follow signboards). The Craw is a charming country inn in the sleepy hamlet of Auchencrow. Auchencrow is famous for its witches – the last witch executed in Britain was from Auchencrow and it is said she still haunts The Craw. This neat detached whitewashed building in the main street has rather small public rooms but these enhance the atmosphere by giving it a homely village pub feel. Best summed up as simple, unpretentious, attentive and friendly.
Proprietor: R A Dickson

SHIP HOTEL
**Harbour Road
Eyemouth
Berwickshire
TD14 5HT
Tel: 08907 50224**

From A1, 1½ miles, on the harbour front. A small friendly hotel on the harbour front of this well known fishing village where, from the pleasant beer garden, you can watch the fishing boats come in. The hotel consists of a recently upgraded lounge bar and public bar. There are also four comfortable letting bedrooms and a pleasant dining room. Ample car parking is available. A popular venue with both locals and visitors alike makes this a worthwhile

diversion off the A1. Home-made bar food is available all day, and being where it is there is naturally emphasis on seafood. A word of warning!!! The ghost of an ex-landlord is reputed to haunt the cellar calling "Time" by switching off the gas cylinders and other strange happenings at the former closing time of 10 pm!
**Alloa Brewery
Tenant: Andy Anderson**

FALKIRK

WHEATSHEAF INN
**16 Baxter's Wynd
Falkirk FK1 1PF
Tel: 0324 23716**

The Wheatsheaf is one of the oldest pubs in town and though it has no adjacent car park it is only one minute's walk from the shops. It is a busy friendly pub with lots of talk and a good atmosphere. Perhaps it earns special credit from having no TV, pool table or one armed bandits. The menu is basic but what is done is of good standard. The haggis, turnip and potato pie is especially tasty. There is an excellent range of beers and lagers and a superb stock of spirits. This is what a pub should be – a good atmosphere, good company and a feeling of being welcome.
Proprietor: Wallace Brown

FALKLAND

THE COVENANTER HOTEL
**The Square
Falkland
Fife KY7 7BU
Tel: 0337 57224**

The Covenanter Hotel is on the picturesque square of this historic village which was built around 16th century Falkland Palace, a favourite royal residence of James V and his daughter, Mary, Queen of Scots. This old coaching inn oozes friendly hospitality and provides an excellent standard of food both in its restaurant and in the food and wine bistro where the atmosphere is less formal.

The timbered ceilings, the style of furnishings, all reflect the character of this two storey stone building dating from 1717. The pleasant service and the standard of food have made the Covenanter a popular place with locals and tourists alike. Falkland is a tourist attraction in Fife because of the Palace and the Covenanter Hotel is exactly the sort of place you would hope to find in a little village like this. Note it is closed on Mondays.

Proprietor : George Menzies

FOCHABERS

RED LION TAVERN

65-67 High Street
Fochabers
Moray

Tel: 0343 820145

On A96, halfway between Aberdeen and Inverness.

The Red Lion Tavern is near the centre of this charming village on the banks of the River Spey which is famous for its salmon fishing. The exterior is attractive with its canopies over entrance and windows and the bars are pleasingly furnished and manned by cheerful staff. It is a traditional Scottish bar with prints and several antique collectors items, in copper and brass, of interest. There is a garden lounge at rear. It serves good home-made food, fresh local produce being used wherever possible. A speciality is Spey salmon during the fishing season.

Proprietor : Keith Smith

FORRES

RAMNEE HOTEL

Victoria Road
Forres
Morayshire
IV36 0BN

Tel: 0309 72410

From the shopping area at the east end of Forres, 500 yards.

Formerly a private house, the Ramnee has been tastefully and carefully transformed to create an interesting small hotel. The building retains many of the original features of craftsmanship rarely found today. An impressive pitch pine lined foyer leads on to a charming cocktail bar where an extensive range of lunches and suppers are served daily, or a place to relax with a cocktail before sampling the excellent French and traditional cuisine in the restaurant. The hotel has 20 bedrooms, all of which have private facilities, and for those wishing to spread out a little, deluxe rooms offer exceptional comfort at reasonable prices. The Ramnee has an award winning reputation for hospitality and service. Everything about this establishment looks right and feels right. One for the 'not to be missed' list.

Proprietor : RJ Dinnes

FORT WILLIAM

MARINERS WINE BAR

The Moorings Hotel
Banavie, Fort William
Inverness-shire
PH33 7LY

Tel: 0397 7 797

On B8004, 8 miles from Fort William.
Based on a nautical theme Mariners Wine Bar at the Moorings is an interesting place to visit with many unusual touches. This cellar bar is full of character, with real oak panelling incorporated in the design from another waterside establishment, an old bank in Leith, Edinburgh's dockside. To accompany a satisfying bar meal, you can choose from an extensive wine list or the

wide selection of spirits, continental beers and lagers, on offer. This is primarily an evening rendezvous but it caters also for bar lunches from 12 to 2.30 pm during the main holiday season (April to October). Suppers 6.30 to 9 pm. Mariners was a finalist in the Guinness Bar Design Awards 1989.
Proprietor: N J A Sinclair

WEST END HOTEL
Fort William
Inverness-shire
Tel: 0397 2614

Originally an old temperance hotel which has had successive improvements and additions, the most recent of which is a striking glass patio. Conveniently sited and very well furnished this is an establishment that will appeal to most people. Although a hotel its handsome bar areas make it also recognisably a pub. An exacting inspector waxed quite lyrical about it and it is clearly a very well managed place with high standards. The bar menu has been planned to appeal to a wide range of clients. Comfortable bedrooms offer the normal facilities expected today.
Proprietor: Mrs M Chisholm

GAIRLOCH

THE OLD INN
Gairloch
Ross-shire
IV21 2BD
Tel: 0445 2006

100 yards off A832 at the harbour end of Gairloch beside the old Flowerdale Footbridge.
Gairloch is only seven miles from the famous sub-tropical gardens at Inverewe, so is very much on the route of anyone travelling north or south along the spectacular west coast of Scotland. The Old Inn is one of those unchanging traditional coaching inns with a relaxing unhurried air. Bar snacks are adequate and interesting and there are facilities for children. The dining room offers an extensive menu of good

fresh produce, specialising in local shellfish and salmon etc. Friendly owners, friendly staff. Comfortable well appointed bedrooms most with en suite bath or shower. A place to stay a while or certainly stop off at for a meal.
Proprietor: David Carruthers

GARVALD

GARVALD HOTEL
Garvald
Nr Haddington
East Lothian
EH41 4LN
Tel: 062 083 229

West of Haddington, 5 miles. This is a good village pub, small but with a good atmosphere and well integrated into village life, though visitors would be made welcome and would not feel out of place. It is set in the very picturesque village of Garvald on the main street at the end of a terraced row of cottages, and it has a small beer garden where the occasional barbecue is held. A bar snack menu is available all day with a more extensive grill menu in the evening. Prices are modest. There are bedrooms with TV and tea making facilities, and children – and well behaved dogs – are welcome.
Proprietor: T M H Butler

GATEHEAD

OLD ROME FARMHOUSE
Gatehead
By Kilmarnock
Ayrshire
KA2 9AJ
Tel: 0563 850265

Situated off A759 to Troon.
Extremely attractive converted farm buildings in white and green set in a handsome farmyard with numerous trees and flowers. It is furnished in farmhouse style and immediately makes you feel a guest of the farmer rather than an impersonal customer. There is a lounge bar with log fire and a separate dining room. Food may be taken in either. The menu is

not extensive but is imaginative and modestly priced. This is a family run establishment that gives every impression of being looked after with loving care and with a keen desire to ensure the comfort and satisfaction of guests.
Proprietors : Mr & Mrs A Elliot

GIRVAN

KING'S ARMS HOTEL

**Dalrymple Street
Girvan
Ayrshire
KA26 9AE
Tel: 0465 3322**

A fine 17th century coaching inn standing at the north end of the main shopping street and close to the harbour. In a county with more than its fair share of world renowned golf courses, it is perhaps somewhat natural that the Bunker Bar has a golfing theme and a unique bar looking like a giant golf ball. Girvan, of course, is in the heart of Burns country. Whether the Bard ever drank at the King's Arms is not recorded but certainly Keats and Wordsworth stayed there. The bar snack menu is fairly limited but is available all day and is reasonably priced. There is an attractive Coachlamp Restaurant. With 25 en suite bedrooms the hotel has much to offer and is very much a family run establishment.
Proprietor : J J Morton & Co

GLASGOW

THE ADMIRAL

**72a Waterloo Street
Glasgow G2 2DA
Tel: 041 221 7705**

This is a good city centre pub in a commercial area with an attractive wood and old world smoked glass entrance. It is situated near Anderston Bus Station within easy walking distance of the busy shopping area of Argyle Street. As the name suggests it has a strong nautical theme. There is a long bar with a dining area at the rear and a lounge bar in the basement. It has been carefully furnished and is well maintained. A warm homely pub that should appeal to most tastes.
Alloa Brewery

ATHOLL ARMS

**134 Renfield Street
Glasgow G2 3AU
Tel: 041 332 5265**

A bar/diner on the ground floor of a city centre block close to the main Sauchiehall Street shopping area, the Theatre Royal and Scottish Television. This is not a fussy or pretentious pub but a straightforward honest establishment providing what its customers want. Food of one kind or another is available virtually all day from noon with lunch being the main event but with an ongoing snack menu from 5 pm till midnight. This is very much a haunt of local business community, staff of STV etc with whom it is popular and convenient.
Welcome Inns

BJ's BAR & DINER

**828 Crow Road
Anniesland Cross
Glasgow G13 1HA**

Situated on Anniesland Cross on the north side of A82. Entry to parking is gained from first right on Bearsden Road (A739).
A good modern city pub with a friendly atmosphere in a bright and comfortable lounge bar standing at what has been described as Scotland's busiest crossroads. It offers good wholesome Scottish fare to the traveller en route to Loch Lomond, the north or the Trossachs. The menu is limited and simple but food is available almost all day from 11.30 am to 6 pm and prices are most reasonable. A happy good natured staff does much to contribute to the pleasant relaxed feeling of the place.
Proprietor : Jack Hutton

THE BANK

**35-41 Queen Street
Glasgow G1 3ED
Tel: 041 221 7926**

Centrally located just by George Square and within easy walking distance from Glasgow's Queen Street Station.

An appealing entrance seems to act as a magnet for the local professional and business community. There is a lounge and dining area on two levels on the ground floor and a basement restaurant. Excellent use has been made of wood panelling in the lounge with an interesting assortment of artefacts. The staff are polite, cheerful and well turned out. There is a good standard of food at reasonable prices. A visit to this Bank might repay your investment!
Alloa Brewery

THE BEECHWOOD
**156 Ardmay Crescent
Kings Park
Glasgow G44 4PP
Tel: 041 632 5476**

A bright, clean, cheerful and welcoming pub located on south side of the River Clyde near Scotland's national football ground, Hampden. With three bars there is a friendly community atmosphere. Good inexpensive food in the bars and a separate restaurant with a more extensive menu concentrating on fresh produce all of which is well presented. Clearly a well patronised, well run pub with something for everyone.
Alloa Brewery

THE BELFRY
**652 Argyle Street
Glasgow G3 8UF
Tel: 041 221 0630**

Situated in the basement of Glasgow's famous Buttery Restaurant. An outstandingly good and extremely popular wine bar serving excellent food, Monday to Friday, lunch and dinner, and Saturday evening dinner. Sharing the kitchen with its famous upstairs neighbour the Buttery, guests can be assured of a first class quality menu at wine bar prices. Easy parking for a city centre establishment. The wine list complements the menu extremely well and does not make the experience a painful one by way of cost! Extremely busy – booking almost essential, but if you don't make it first time, keep on trying. It is well worth the effort.
Alloa Brewery

BOBOLOVSKY'S BALLOON
**88 Mitchell Street
Glasgow G1 3NA
Tel: 041 221 0333**

This interestingly named pub is well-known in Glasgow. The interior is a cacophany of oversize bric-a-brac and has a lot of interesting features. It all blends well and creates a nice 'yuppie' type atmosphere. For such a modern well thought out interior, our inspector felt the menu was very average. Food is only available during lunchtime. However the cheerful staff and the service combine with the high bar standards to make this a place to visit in the city centre.
Proprietors : Mr & Mrs R Thomson

THE BRASSERIE
**176 West Regent Street
Glasgow G2 4RL
Tel: 041 248 3801**

2 minutes walk from Blythswood Square, on left hand side down West Regent Street. Recently refurbished to a high standard the Brasserie, West Regent Street, has developed from customer pressure in its sister establishment, Rogano/Cafe Rogano, for a quality eating house at the 'top of the town'. A simple, but exciting cafe/brasserie menu has captured the attention of the West of Scotland eating public, and already in its early days it is proving to be an extremely popular venue. Open Monday to Saturday 12 noon till late. Right in the city centre it has a wide and varied clientele and with high standards seems determined to keep them.
Alloa Brewery

CAFE ROGANO
**11 Exchange Place
Glasgow G1 3AN
Tel: 041 248 4913**

Situated beneath Rogano Restaurant in Exchange Place off Buchanan Street. Rogano's in Glasgow is almost an institution patronised and loved by one generation after another. One would therefore expect that its downstairs operation, Cafe Rogano, would excel. It does. Cafe Rogano is the setting for less formal dining than in Rogano itself, with a fresh and original menu, and lots of atmosphere. Open throughout the day, it is ideal for catching up with lunch after a shopping trip or for a pre-theatre dinner or after-theatre supper. Cheerful, efficient staff make it all a pleasurable experience.
Alloa Brewery

CORN EXCHANGE
**88 Gordon Street
Glasgow G1 3AP
Tel: 041 248 5380**

Directly opposite Glasgow's Central Station.
One of Glasgow's oldest pubs. Though recently refurbished, it still retains its unique character. Popular with tourists, but really a pub for all the general public. There is a limited menu of popular inexpensive dishes and the standard is good. A warm and inviting pub right in the heart of the city. Good value for money.
Alloa Brewery

DE QUINCEY'S
**Renfield Street
Glasgow
Tel: 041 333 0633**

On corner of Renfield Street and West Regent Street.
Located on the ground floor of an impressive red sandstone building in the centre of Glasgow, De Quincey's definitely has a style of its own. There is a touch of the orient about the place with its lofty ceilings, high archways and overhead ceiling fans. The wicker furniture, potted palms etc are entirely in keeping with the character as are the magnificent tiled walls and pillars. All blend to create a cool oasis of comfort. Food is available until mid afternoon, and it is renowned for its cocktail list. The staff are young and lively. Their friendly attitude makes your visit a memorable one.

THE DOUBLET BAR
**74 Park Road
Glasgow G4 9JF
Tel: 041 334 1982**

Junction of Woodlands Road and Park Road - close proximity to Glasgow University.
A typical Glasgow pub with its public bar in mock Tudor style decor and an oak panelled lounge bar upstairs with its own entrance in South Woodside Road. It is close to Glasgow University and Queen's College, offering a wide range of beers including McEwan's 80/-, Younger's No 3 and Belhaven 80/- real ales. The clientele is a good cross-section representation of the city ranging from students to writers, artists, business and professional people. A modest choice of bar snacks is available throughout opening hours.
**Proprietors : Mr A M Don
& Mrs M A L Young**

DOW'S
**9-11 Dundas Street
Glasgow G1 2AN
Tel: 041 332 7935**

Take the side exit from Queen Street Station and you are at Dow's. This pub with its attractive frontage is just the place to relax before or after a train journey but is also a good place to eat. There is a certain old world charm in the interior style of the place with its wood panelled walls, pictures and artefacts. Food is relatively simple but of a good standard and well presented. A warm and welcoming pub with a congenial atmosphere.
Alloa Brewery

EXCHEQUER

**59 Dumbarton Road
Glasgow G11 6PD
Tel: 041 334 3301**

Approximately 400 yards west of Kelvin Hall Sports Arena.
Licensee, Jack Kinnell, has transformed these premises into a celebration of the great Victorian style of Glasgow. It is a large pub with a saloon bar and lounge bar on the ground floor and another lounge area upstairs. Its freshly prepared menu is served throughout the day until 9 pm. The Exchequer also has a beer garden at the rear of the premises, an extremely important facility in this area, so close to the Western Infirmary and Medical College. Live entertainment is a popular Sunday evening event. A full range of Alloa ales and lagers is available.
**Alloa Brewery
Tenant : Jack Kinnell**

FINLAY'S

**137 Kilmarnock Road
Shawlands
Glasgow
Tel: 041 632 9939**

Opposite Shawlands Shopping Centre. Finlay's is situated in a refurbished beige sandstone tenement building on the main shopping street in Shawlands, on the south side of Glasgow. It is a well established single bar operation, offering a wide selection of bar snacks and full meals. The food is of a good standard and well presented it is available from noon till 7.30 pm Monday to Friday, and till 5.30 pm on Saturday. Finlay's is also open 11.30 am until 2 pm on a Sunday for 'late breakfast'. An interesting range of 'Southsiders' frequent this friendly local hostelry.
Tennents Taverns

GLASGOW BRASSERIE

**22-24 West Nile Street
Glasgow
Tel: 041 221 8044**

This is one of the newest bar restaurants to appear on the Glasgow scene and it is a winner. There is a splendid atmosphere to it both in the brasserie on the ground floor and the elegant restaurant downstairs. It is clearly a busy and popular rendezvous at lunchtime for the local business community and shoppers. The menu is excellent with a number of unusual dishes, all very well presented and first class value, and the service lives up to the high standards of the food. There is much to commend this place. It is a top class brasserie operation with a high reputation.
Proprietor : Beard Hotels Ltd

THE GRANARY

**10-16 Kilmarnock Road
Glasgow G2 3JD
Tel: 041 632 8487**

There is always a buzz of excitement and a really lively atmosphere in this well-known bar and diner much frequented by Glasgow's trendies. It attracts a good clientele, there with their friends or to meet new ones. The staff is as vivacious as the place itself. The food is of high standard and is well presented. If you do not live there, it is well worth the trip to Shawlands to experience the Granary. This pub is almost certain to appeal to you.
Alloa Brewery

HANRAHANS

**16 Nicholson Street
Glasgow G5 9TR
Tel: 041 420 1069**

This is an interesting operation on three floors with a fine atmosphere and an exclusive feel to it. There is a bar on the ground floor and small intimate dining rooms on the first and second floors, and the clientele seems to cover all age groups and professions. Trade is primarily lunchtime 12 to 2.30 pm and evening 6 to 9.30 pm (last orders). Wherever possible fresh produce is used and food quality is of

high standard. The staff respond to the quality of the surroundings and are quick, efficient and politely cheerful. Overall, this is a small intimate and high class establishment, well managed, well maintained and well worthy of recognition.
Proprietor: The McFarlane Group

LOCK 27
**1100 Crow Road
Anniesland
Glasgow G13 1XX
Tel: 041 958 0853**

As the name implies, this recently built pub stands at Lock 27 on the Forth and Clyde Canal with car parking alongside and a beer garden at the water's edge. Tasteful decoration and quality furnishings contribute to the splendid atmosphere and there is a superb range of good food, and drink of every kind. You can enjoy steak and Guinness pie or chargrilled swordfish steaks – something you don't find in every pub and, weather permitting, you can eat al fresco. Pub lunches are particularly popular here. Open seven days a week, food is served from noon to 5 pm Monday to Wednesday and till 8 pm Thursday (12.30 to 4 pm Sundays). This is a very good pub indeed. Well cared for with beautifully presented food and excellent standards of service.
Proprietor: H McLean

MAXWELL'S
**Pollokshaws Road
Glasgow G42
Tel: 041 632 9048**

The famous Marlborough function rooms at Shawlands are well-known to generations of Glaswegians and Maxwell's bar is a contiguous operation. Recently refurbished, there is a fine spacious feel to the place and the decor is striking and somewhat unusual. This is primarily a cafe bar establishment and it appears to be aiming at a higher market level than may have been the situation in the past. It gives every indication of being well maintained and well managed and is a pleasant and relaxing place in which to enjoy a quiet and enjoyable hour or two with friends.
Proprietor: Stakis plc

THE MITRE BAR
**12 Brunswick Street
Glasgow G1 1TD
Tel: 041 552 3764**

In lane diagonally opposite C & A Modes, Trongate, Glasgow city centre.
Unspoilt small Victorian pub tucked up an alley off Trongate shopping area. Only a walk from train station on Argyle Street and underground at St Enoch Square. Pub food available all day. Open 11 am to 11 pm. Closed Sundays. Real ale on draught (Belhaven 80/- and 60/-). Marvellous selection of malt whiskies. A warm congenial and inviting little pub neither pretentious nor stuffy with value for money food and drink.
Proprietor: P Raymond McCrudden

NAPOLEON'S
**128 Merrylee Road
Glasgow
Tel: 041 637 5238**

Leave Glasgow by Kilmarnock road and turn left at Merrylee.
From all accounts Napoleon Bonaparte had an impressive frontage. So does this Napoleon's on the south side of the city, sympathetically converted from a famous Glasgow bakery. Inside there is a large circular bar with a disco dance floor and a separate dining area. Main meals are served from noon to 2.30 pm and from 6 to 9.30 pm with snacks in the in between period. Fresh food is used where possible and the food is of high standard. Service is first class. Good quality furnishings are evident throughout and public areas are maintained well. Napoleon's is an interesting and attractive establishment catering for all age groups though a younger clientele predominates at night.
Tennents Taverns

PARTICK TAVERN
**163-169 Dumbarton Road
Glasgow G60 5JQ
Tel: 041 339 7571**

This traditionally furnished lounge bar is situated close to some of Glasgow's most interesting venues including the Kelvin Hall Sports Arena, Transport Museum, Art

Gallery and the more modern, Scottish Exhibition Centre. Amongst the bric-a-brac on display is a unique collection of Glasgow scenes dating back to the turn of the century which is sure to create interest. Good home-cooked bar food utilising fresh produce as much as possible throughout the day and evening. There is a comfortable and pleasant atmosphere here and you can also enjoy some of the best of typical Glasgow humour.
Alloa Brewery

PIAF'S BRASSERIE
87 Kilmarnock Road
Shawlands
Glasgow G1 3BU
Tel: 041 649 3141

Piaf's Brasserie on the south side of Glasgow needs no gimmicks to keep it in the news. It usually manages to be there of a right. Its most recent achievement was to win first prize in the Guinness Design Awards 1989 and a visit to this most attractive pub will quickly demonstrate the reason. Jack Flanagan, the owner, has created a fashionable elegant establishment of high standard with a skilful use of space and materials. This is deservedly a very popular rendezvous with a growing reputation for excellence.
Proprietor: Mr J Flanagan

PIER 39
Customs House Quay
Glasgow G1 4JJ
Tel: 041 221 0021

There is a delightful, airy, open atmosphere in this place with glimpses of sun, sky, river and trees – almost the impression of being aboard a ship. It occupies a new glass building on the Clyde walkway adjacent to the main shopping area and the St Enoch indoor shopping complex. It caters for almost everyone, though probably the younger set predominates in the evenings and at weekends. There is excellent food well presented and a good accompanying wine list. Bar lunches are at normal times of noon to 2.30 pm Monday to Saturay while the restaurant is open for lunch at the same time and in the evening from 6 to 11 pm.

Quality furniture and furnishings contribute to the thoroughly pleasing overall appearance with Morgan's Landing restaurant being particularly appealing. Staff, reception and service rise to the heights of the surroundings. A first class enjoyable experience for anyone.
Proprietor: The McFarlane Group

THE PLACE
23 Sandyford Place
Glasgow G3 7NG
Tel: 041 221 0770

At west end of Sauchiehall Street, near Charing Cross.
The Place is a bar and steakhouse operation situated in the basement and ground floor of a sandstone building in treelined Sandyford Place, on Sauchiehall Street. There is an excellent atmosphere and It appeals to a mixed age group. The bar serves food from noon till 3 pm and from 5 till 10 pm. The steakhouse hours are noon to 3 pm and 6 pm to 11 pm. Clever use of mirrors in the public areas and tastefully decorated. Warm and friendly service make this a popular rendezvous.
Proprietor: James Monaghan

RABHA'S
83 Hutcheson Street
Glasgow G1 1SH
Tel: 041 553 1545

Unless you are a Scot you may well wonder what language and nationality you are trying to identify in this unusually named pub, but Rab Ha, it is said, was the original 'Glasgow Glutton'. This is really more of a pub restaurant than a straightforward pub and its superb quality of food and excellent service draw people from all over the city. It occupies the ground floor and basement of an old building in Hutcheson Street and has earned itself a high reputation. The bar is traditional rather than exceptional and has its own menu, but the restaurant with its emphasis on good Scottish fare and seafood is special. Try the Loch Fyne oysters...A very good establishment.
Proprietors: Alasdair & Ann Hopkins

THE ROCK
205 Hyndland Road
Glasgow G12 8EZ
Tel: 041 334 6977

A free standing modern building in the west end of this superior residential area, with a small garden around it and adequate car parking to the rear. It has been luxuriously equipped with good quality furnishings and is maintained to a high standard. Well presented good wholesome food makes it a popular lunch place and there is a special brunch on Sundays. There is a feeling of warmth and airiness to the Rock from the moment you cross the door and the general ambience is very pleasing. This is a first class local residential and passers-by pub, well run and kept in near immaculate condition.
Proprietor: Stakis plc

SCARAMOUCHE
140 Elderslie Street
Glasgow G3 7AW
Tel: 041 333 9735

Situated in Elderslie Street, 100 yards from Charing Cross.
The big oblong bar which always seems to be bustling gives warmth and atmosphere to this city centre pub in the middle of the commercial area. Bar snacks at normal prices are available from noon to 10 pm, while the Conservatory Restaurant has a more extensive a la carte menu. The clientele is mixed, tending on the younger side, and the staff of many local offices find this a convenient watering hole at lunchtime and a place to pop into before going home in the evenings. A genuine and attractive city pub manned by a cheerful capable staff.
Welcome Inns

SLOANS
Argyll Arcade
62 Argyle Street
Glasgow G2 8AG
Tel: 041 221 8917

Sloan's claims to be Glasgow's oldest restaurant and its Victorian grandeur has been undiminished by the passage of time. It is located on the first and second floors above the shops in this famous shopping arcade. There are wood panelled walls and good quality furnishings, and a limited menu of well presented food with an emphasis on fresh produce. Inexpensive. Children welcome.
Alloa Brewery

STIRLING CASTLE BAR
90 Old Dumbarton Road
Glasgow G3 8AQ
Tel: 041 339 8132

Recent and very effective renovation of the outside of this corner site makes an immediate impact. Equally pleasing is the re-designed interior which is very bright and airy. What is done here is done well and this is apparent, too, in the menu which is extensive but avoids being too adventurous. Food is available all day till 10 pm and is good value. Good management is apparent in the way in which public areas are maintained. The decor, the standard of service and the atmosphere make this an excellent local well worth a visit be you local or visitor – even just for the food.
Proprietor : Andrew Main

THE THIRTY-NINE STEPS
95 Union Street
Glasgow G1
Tel: 041 221 5020

A magnificent marble staircase leads into this outstandingly good family run establishment. It is centrally situated, virtually under Glasgow Central Station and adjacent to the east entrance. Internally the atmosphere is superb. Good use has been made of stained glass on the gantry with raised floor levels on either side of the long bar. Separate restaurant interestingly styled like the Forth Railway Bridge. There is an unusually wide range of home and overseas beers, some 60 wines, and around 65 malts on offer. Food from an extensive menu is superbly presented and is available from 11 am to 10 pm. The premises have been designed with taste and furnished with quality materials. The welcome is warm, cheerful and genuine. By any measurement this is an absolutely top class pub, reflecting

the greatest credit on its management and setting a fine example to the trade. Positively one not to be missed.
Proprietors : The Waterson Family

TIMES SQUARE
**40-48 St Enoch Square
Glasgow G1 4DH
Tel: 041 221 6579**

Directly opposite Glasgow's newest shopping arcade this interesting American style bar/diner offers the unusual in its young lively theme bar. There is a well-appointed bar with a raised dining area at the rear and a good selection of ales and lagers together with the usual range of spirits and wines. A good standard of straightforward unpretentious - and inexpensive – food is available at lunchtime and in the evenings. A pub that offers the public nice surroundings, good value food and drink – and the occasional zany party night.
Alloa Brewery

THE TRADING POST
**63 Carlton Place
Glasgow G5 9TR
Tel: 041 429 3445**

This is an interesting basement bar restaurant adjacent to the suspension bridge over the River Clyde and close to the huge St Enoch shopping complex. It has an American wild west theme with a log cabin decor and good, if basic, furniture in keeping with the theme. A lot of care and attention is devoted to the food, with lunches from 12 to 3 pm and evening meals from 6 pm to midnight weekdays (6.30 to 11 pm Sundays). There is concentration on the use of fresh local produce wherever possible and good presentation. There is a separate room for children eating with adults, and it is pleasing to see an interesting establishment of this type welcoming family groups. This is a good theme pub, interestingly different, and offering excellent food and an enjoyable meal experience.
Proprietor : The McFarlane Group

UBIQUITOUS CHIP
**12 Ashton Lane
Glasgow G12 8SJ
Tel: 041 334 7109**

The Ubiquitous Chip is almost an institution in Glasgow with an outstanding reputation and its Chip Bar shares in the glory. An unpretentious pub where regulars sit around the peat fire playing backgammon. The Chip Bar is a busy haven for university and media folk. Draught beers – Furstenberg and Caledonian are unpasteurised – and 14 wines are available by the glass at very reasonable prices. All spirits including an exceptional range of malt whiskies are available in the traditional Scots $1/4$ gill. The Scottish emphasis that made the downstairs restaurant so rightly famous is continued in pub food. Hot dishes such as vegetarian haggis and neeps, mince pie and ham houghs, compete with fresh fish and a large selection of salads made on the premises to give the customer a wide choice of wholesome food for under £5. It opens from 11 am to 11 pm Monday to Saturday and on Sunday from 12.30 to 2.30 pm. By any measure this is a very special establishment.
Proprietor : R Clydesdale

GLENDEVON

TORMAUKIN INN
**Glendevon
By Dollar
Perthshire
FK14 7JY
Tel: 025 981 252**

On A823 between Dunfermline and Crieff or via exits 5, 6 or 7 from M90.
It is well worth anyone's time to drive through Glendevon. It genuinely is an area of outstanding natural beauty and positively a place to stay a while or at least stop for a meal. The Tormaukin dates back nearly 300 years. It has recently been thoroughly – but sensitively – refurbished. Timber ceilings and natural stone reflect the past and add dignity and character to the building, but every modern comfort has also been included. The bedrooms are excellently appointed and all with bathrooms en suite. There are

good bar lunches and suppers and the a la carte restaurant has earned a good reputation. The proprietors and their staff do everything possible to ensure that their guests will want to return.
Proprietors : R S & M C Worthy

GLENSHEE

THE BLACKWATER INN

**Glenshee
Perthshire
PH10 7LH
Tel: 025 085 234**

Roadside A93, 9 miles north of Blairgowrie. 20 miles south of Braemar.
The lounge diner has a huge log fire and entrance to a patio beer garden with over 200 (some rare) Alpine plants in the natural rockery and a delightful natural waterfall. The Old Sawmill Restaurant has natural beams and is in part of the building that began as a sawmill in the 1800s. The fireplace and bar are built of local stone. The bar houses an extremely interesting collection of old saws, cooper tools and joiner planes. Bar meals are served all day until 9 pm with a wide range of main courses on offer along with a complement of starters and sweets. The inn won a 1989 Award of Excellence from Dairy Crest for its cheese selections. The accent is on good food and friendly, efficient, welcoming service. There are nine bedrooms all centrally heated and with tea making facilities. Families are especially welcome.
Proprietor : Ivy Bailey

GOLSPIE

SUTHERLAND ARMS HOTEL

**Old Bank Road
Golspie
Sutherland
KW10 6RS
Tel: 04083 3234/3216**

A handsome stone building at the north end of Golspie with a large car park. It is almost 200 years since the Duke of Sutherland established this hotel as the first coaching inn in Sutherland. Much of the atmosphere of bygone days has been retained though of course it has been modernised over the years to meet the present demands e.g. most of the bedrooms have bathrooms and the usual amenities. The hotel has a good reputation for its food and all main meals are provided plus a good range of bar lunches. There is a more restricted meal service in the winter months when the flow of tourist trade is limited.
Proprietor : Colin Sutherland

GULLANE

QUEENS HOTEL

**Main Street
Gullane
East Lothian
EH31 2AS
Tel: 0620 842275**

A prominent whitewashed building standing in its own grounds and well-known to most people who pass through Gullane. There is an attractive entrance lobby with an open fire and a lounge bar leading from it, and an instantly conveyed impression of a pleasant relaxed atmosphere. Bar lunches are better than average and are well presented. Service is very good. There is also, of course, a separate dining room where standards are equally high. Perhaps it has something to do with the many golfers who find their way here but the excellent toilets even have showers! All in all this is a welcoming and pleasant hotel with a good reputation and good standards.
Proprietor : Ann B Robertson

HAMILTON

THE GEORGE BAR
**Campbell Street
Hamilton**

If there were grades for pubs the George in Hamilton would probably fall into the category of a working man's pub – and that is not meant in any derogatory manner because such pubs are the very core of the trade. The George is not pretentious; it does not make the mistake of pretending to be what it is not, but there is a lot of attraction to it. It is crisp and clean. The base of old whisky barrels, brass plates, horse brasses and old gas style light fitments etc have been used to give the place character. Bar lunches and snacks are simple but satisfactory and meet the needs of the customers. This is a good example of a good local which clearly appeals to its regulars and would be found equally pleasing by visitors.
Proprietor : Colin Wiseman Inns Ltd

THE STONEHOUSE BAR
**45 Cadzow Street
Hamilton
Tel: 0698 286479**

A very bright and well furnished pub of good external appearance. It is on a main thoroughfare and unfortunately lacks an immediate car park. Not that this deters its clientele who are primarily local and well-known to the proprietors. A limited snack menu is available in the bar between 12 noon and 3 pm, very modestly priced. Service is good and the staff are cheerful and popular. Public areas are well furnished and maintained to a very high standard. There is a good family atmosphere about this place. It is highly popular locally, and is clearly well managed and controlled.
Proprietor : James Monaghan

HOUSTON

FOX & HOUNDS
**South Street
Houston
Renfrewshire
PA6 7EN
Tel: 0505 612448**

From Glasgow Airport, 6 miles.
This looks and is very much a traditional and delightful old hostelry in a country village. There are three separate bars, equipped to a high standard of comfort and looked after by a well trained professional staff. Meals are available up to 10 pm with good quality bar snacks and a full a la carte menu in the Huntsman Restaurant. The management is alert and capable – and it shows. Everything is well maintained and well cared for. A really first class pub which has something for all age groups and which should satisfy most, if not all of them.
Proprietor : Ronald Wengel

INVERARAY

THE GEORGE HOTEL
**Main Street East
Inveraray
PA32 8TT
Tel: 0499 2111**

A fine old three storey building, built over 200 years ago and dominating the main street. Hanging baskets of flowers and colourful window boxes make a vivid splash against the white stonework. The interior exudes the atmosphere of the past, especially in the George Bar with its old flagstones and a peat or log fire burning. There is an interesting range of bar snacks available and a tastefully decorated panelled dining room for more formal eating. The hotel has earned a well deserved reputation for its food, and makes maximum use of the

excellent fish and shellfish obtained locally. The staff are polite, attentive and efficient, and the building is well equipped and well maintained. This is a fine old hotel the sort of place that is the social heart of the community. It is full of character and of interest and stands out from its competitors like a standard bearer.
Proprietor : Donald Clark

INVERNESS

BRAHAN SEER
**Balnafettack Road
Inverness
Tel: 0463 243111**

The Brahan Seer is the highest pub in Inverness with superb views across the town and the Firth. Built only three years ago, the pub has a comfortable lounge/dining room and ample parking. The interior is furnished in modern style with cane backed chairs and is bright and airy with lots of window tables. The dominant situation of this pub is almost good enough reason alone to pay a visit. But there is more to it than that. It is well equipped, has a good atmosphere, and a good selection of keg beers and food.
Tennents Taverns

CRAIGMONIE HOTEL
**9 Annfield Road
Inverness
IV2 3HX
Tel: 0463 231649**

Top of Castle Street, left into Old Edinburgh Road. At traffic lights go forward into Annfield Road.
Located a few minutes walk from the centre of Inverness the Craigmonie was built for William MacKay, a lawyer and Gaelic scholar, whose great grandfather fought alongside Bonnie Prince Charlie at Culloden in 1746. This is a splendidly equipped town house hotel, owned and managed by the Moffat family who have skilfully blended historic tradition with modern style to produce a delightful luxurious hotel. The comfortable wood panelled Jacobite Lounge Bar offers a wide choice of lunch and supper dishes concentrating on quality and featuring many traditional Scottish recipes. Chef de Cuisine Moffat (second son of the family and business partner) presides over the kitchen which also serves the Darnaway Restaurant offering formal dining from table d'hote and a la carte menus. The hotel has 35 rooms en suite with poolside suites adjoining a new state of the art leisure sportif. A thoroughly modern hotel with lots of amenities, and likely to satisfy the most fastidious whether for a bar lunch or a several days stay.
Proprietors : The Moffat Family

FINLAY'S
**Tomnahurich Street
Inverness
Tel: 0463 231335**

On the fringe of the shopping area. Over the river – one minute's walk from Town Hall. Tucked away from the busy town centre, Finlay's offers a traditional haven in which to enjoy a meal and a relaxing drink. The frontage of this pub is extremely smart and no expense has been spared on the interior either. There are lovely brass fittings on the bar and a split level seating area which is warm and friendly and furnished in dark wood. Varied menu available at lunchtimes all week and Sunday lunches are a speciality. Suppers are served 5.30 pm to 8.30 pm during the week. Children under 12 are not admitted. Not catering for someone in a hurry – more a relaxed experience. There is a good range of keg and cask conditioned ales. This pub is popular and attracts a good mix of locals and visitors alike.
Tennents Taverns

GLEN MHOR HOTEL
**9-12 Ness Bank
Inverness
IV2 4SG
Tel: 0463 234308**

On the south bank of the River Ness, below the castle.
The Glen Mhor is a privately owned and directed traditional style of hotel with all modern facilities. In addition to its comfortable bedrooms, it is a free house with three bars and a restaurant. Nico's Bistro Bar – very much an intimate continental

atmosphere with soft lighting, alcoves and gingham tablecloths. Italian specialities are served all year round, lunchtimes and evenings. Inexpensive Scottish specialities served throughout the summer months. Nicky Tams Pub – refurbished 18th century stables, with log fire, real ale, light snacks, pool and darts. Nico's and Nicky Tams share a patio for summer 'al fresco' dining and wining. The Cocktail Lounge – with an extensive range of malt whiskies is ideal for a quiet chat or aperitif before enjoying a 'Modern Taste of Scotland' dinner in the Riverview Restaurant. This is a very popular and very well managed establishment with smart attentive staff, a place for everyone to enjoy.
Proprietor : J Nicol Manson

HAUGHDALE HOTEL
**19 Ness Bank
Inverness
IV2 4SF
Tel: 0463 233065**

On the banks of the River Ness just five minutes walk from Inverness Town Centre this old country house has been converted over the years to a hotel. This is the sort of quiet restful place to which people return year after year. There is no hustle or bustle, no pinball machines, just a quiet friendly and helpful staff out to make you feel relaxed. The menu is traditional and unpretentious but reasonably priced. This is a solid dependable establishment with no frills which may not appeal to young go-getters but would be a peaceful haven for those who take life in a less hectic style. It is a quiet residential hotel with beautiful walks along the river.
Proprietor: A Sutherland

HEATHMOUNT HOTEL
**Kingsmills Road
Inverness
IV2 3JN
Tel: 0463 235877**

An attractive Victorian building in a select area of Inverness yet only two to three minutes from the main shopping centre and with its own large car park. There are little touches of Victoriana in the interior where the open plan bar is informal and relaxed. There is a limited but adequate menu with good size portions and reasonable prices. This is a well-run friendly pub catering for all ages, including children, and with attentive and caring staff.
Proprietors : Patrick & Fiona Buxton

INCHMORE HOTEL
**Kirkhill
By Inverness
IV5 7PX
Tel: 0463 83240/83296**

On A862 coast road to Beauly 6 miles west of Inverness.
Originally a coaching inn with a history going back at least to the 16th century the hotel has been tastefully redecorated and upgraded by its current owners who pride themselves in offering good quality food (bar meals and restaurant) in a friendly relaxed atmosphere. The hotel was closely associated with the smugglers of the illicit whisky distilled in the Inverness district until the end of the 19th century and there are many tales associated with these times. With its setting just west of Inverness the Inchmore Hotel forms an excellent base for touring Glen Affric, the west and north, Speyside, the Cairngorms, the Whisky Trail and the beautiful Moray coast. Facilities in the area include golf, fishing, shooting, riding and hill walking. There are seven rooms, all en suite with colour TV, direct dial telephones and tea/coffee making facilities. Although a little out of Inverness, this is a smart clean hotel well worth a visit for its home-cooking and 'no hassle' atmosphere.
Proprietor: Alastair Mackay

INNES BAR
**61 Innes Street
Inverness
IV1 1NR
Tel: 0463 232397**

Adjacent to town centre and industrial estate.
A row of cottages has been linked to form this pleasant pub with its well equipped bar and dining and lounge areas. It attracts a good cross-section of customers – local

business people, shoppers and estate workers. It is not a stuffy or pretentious establishment and limits itself to a fairly restricted and simple range of food, served by an alert and attentive staff. A place without frills but well maintained and run to a good standard. It knows its customers and is well supported by them, which rather speaks for itself.
Welcome Inns

LOCHARDIL HOUSE HOTEL
**Stratherrick Road
Inverness
IV2 4LF
Tel: 0463 235995**

Old family mansion on the outskirts of Inverness. Pleasant, quiet and dignified surroundings, away from the bustle. There is a good trade from business at this hotel and it also meets the demands of the residents in the neighbourhood in which it is situated. There is an adequate menu available and children are welcome for bar meals. The staff are eager and attentive without being pushy. Choice of food may be limited but it is good and well presented. Under such experienced management, it is not surprising that the hotel reflects their high standards and gives every impression of being well supervised.
Proprietor: Mrs E Fraser

MUIRTOWN MOTEL
**11 Clachnaharry Road
Inverness
IV3 6LT
Tel: 0463 243860**

On A862 Dingwall road.
A picturesquely situated motel overlooking the Black Isle and with a delightful open aspect to the Moray Firth, the Muirtown Motel lies on the A862 coastal route north to Beauly and Dingwall. The Muirtown's accommodation has now been extensively modernised to suit the 1990s with the completion of a fine purpose-built bedroom complex containing 20 en suite rooms. You are made welcome here with a friendly, attentive staff reflecting the attitude of the proprietor. A wide range of food, unpretentious but appropriate to local demand is served throughout the day from breakfast at 8 am through to dinner at 9 pm.
Proprietor: George S B MacLean

PHOENIX
**Academy Street
Inverness
Tel: 0463 233685**

With its sawdust flooring, white aproned staff and original atmosphere the Phoenix has been and continues to be almost an institution. It is a warm inviting pub. Food is geared to restaurant service rather than 'pub grub' and there are a lot of nice touches to it. The Phoenix has been nominated by the *Aberdeen Press & Journal* as 'Pub of the Year' and has also earned a CAMRA commendation for the standard of its 'real ales'. Public areas are maintained in superb condition. In the overall assessment of the Phoenix our inspector described it as "an absolute cracker of a pub".
Tennents Taverns

VINES WINE BAR
**Gellions Hotel
10 Bridge Street
Inverness
IV1 1HI
Tel: 0463 233648**

This is the only non smoking wine bar in the Highland capital. A lovely old pub maintained in traditional style to a very high standard. Wood decor and warm colours create a relaxed atmosphere in which to enjoy the interesting home-cooked food. The menu is limited but portions are generous and prices are modest. There is a host of fine wines, spirits or draught bottled beers from which to choose. There is also freshly ground cappuccino, espresso, or regular coffee and a large selection of continental teas anytime of the day. A good rendezvous at any time.
Proprietor: George S B MacLean

IRVINE

MARINA INN
110 Harbour Street
Irvine
KA12 8PZ
Tel: 0294 74079

The Marina Inn is on the waterfront and directly behind the Magnum Centre, Irvine's prestige leisure centre. This modern harbourside bar has an enviable reputation for the seafood served both at lunchtime and in the evenings. A morning coffee served after a walk along the harbourside is a welcome refreshment in a stylish bar. There is a beer garden to the rear where summer barbecues are held. A lively, interesting pub in all senses. Food is of a good standard and very reasonably priced.
Alloa Brewery
Tenant : Mr J Rodger

ISLE OF WHITHORN

THE STEAM PACKET INN
Harbour Row
Isle of Whithorn
Wigtownshire
DG8 8LL
Tel: 098 85 334

This is an idyllic spot and the Steam Packet, right on the waterfront, has been converted with good taste and sensitivity. It must be a delightful base for the yachting fraternity or anyone else interested in the bustle of activity in a busy harbour. The bar is equipped like a sailing ship saloon, is full of interesting pictures and is appropriately furnished. The menu is basic and limited but no doubt is tailored to the needs of the clientele. Bar lunches and bar suppers are available and there is a large selection of filled rolls at very reasonable prices. An additional blackboard menu lists more substantial dishes of the day. The public areas are kept spotlessly clean and are obviously maintained to a high standard. There are lots of things to do in the Isle of Whithorn area besides watching the sea and this very pleasant pub with its cheery staff makes a good place from which to do it. There are rooms with private bathrooms and all facilities.
Proprietors : John & Sarah Scoular

KETTLEBRIDGE

KETTLEBRIDGE INN
9 Cupar Road
Kettlebridge
Fife
KY7 7QD
Tel: 0337 30232

On A92, 2 miles north-east of Glenrothes. Visitors should enjoy a visit to this quaint village pub with its old world coaching inn atmosphere. Exposed stonework and beamed ceilings, horse harness, brass fittings and log fires all combine to create a warm and comfortable feel to the place. It has a reputation for the quality of its real ales and serves palatable and inexpensive good quality bar lunches daily. Evening meals are also available Thursday to Sunday. It is within easy distance of most of the first class golf courses in Fife.
Proprietors : David & Margaret Doig

KILCHRENAN

KILCHRENAN INN
Kilchrenan
Taynuilt
Argyll
PA35 1HD
Tel: 08663 232

Follow the single track B845 from Taynuilt through beautiful Glen Nant for 6 miles. The inn is situated close to the western shore of Loch Awe.
The inn has been completely refurbished recently and the charming interior features a beamed ceiling in the bar with an open log fire. Outside, tables and parasols along the front of the inn along with tubs of flowers and hanging baskets make a most attractive picture. There is an excellent choice of bar snacks and the lunch and dinner menu offers many home-made dishes from the best of local produce. Part of the restaurant is set aside for non smokers. The present building

is approximately 150 years old and is situated close to the original Kilchrenan Inn (now a private home) on the old drovers route from the Highlands and Islands to the Lowland cattle markets. Everything is neat and tidy and well maintained. A place to go back to.

Proprietors : Mr & Mrs Alasdair Scott

KILMARNOCK

THE HUNTING LODGE

**14-16 Glencairn Square
Kilmarnock
KA1 4AH
Tel: 0563 22920**

A handsome modern building occupying a corner site, and with a well appointed and welcoming interior in old oak style. There is a limited but good menu of bar food at reasonable prices available all day and there is a separate dining room for more formal meals. Care is taken with the preparation and presentation of food which is of very good standard and served deftly and cheerfully by the staff. The public areas are kept in the excellent condition you would expect in such a well run establishment. The Hunting Lodge exudes an air of reliability and you would expect standards always to be high.

Tennents Taverns

KILMELFORD

CUILFAIL HOTEL

**Kilmelford
Oban
Argyll
PA34 4XA
Tel: 08522 274**

Situated on A816, 15 miles south of Oban and 26 miles north of Lochgilphead.

One of the nicest old pubs in this lovely part of Argyll. It has retained much of the character and charm of its old coaching days. Directly across the road from it is a spacious and well kept garden – a delightful spot in which to sit and converse over a drink while the sun goes down around you. The Cuilfail bar is very popular and its good home-cooking is clearly appreciated by visitors and locals alike. Quality ingredients are transformed into imaginative meals. There is also a dining room for those looking for a quieter place away from the bustle of the bar, open during the season from Easter to October. Rooms are spacious, some have bathrooms and there are special terms for children sharing with parents.

Proprietors : Mr & Mrs J McFadyen

KINGSEAT

HALFWAY HOUSE HOTEL

**46 Main Street
Kingseat, Dunfermline
Fife
KY12 0TH
Tel: 0383 731661**

Leave M90 at exit 3 by A994 Dunfermline road, then turn first right for Kingseat.

This small family run hotel is situated in the pleasant village of Kingseat, just 30 minutes from Edinburgh and five from Dunfermline. Twelve comfortably furnished bedrooms, all with private bath and shower, remote colour TV, radio, hair dryer and tea/coffee making facilities. The tastefully decorated Burgundy Dining Room is supplemented by delicious bar lunches and suppers. Adjacent to many golf courses, including Gleneagles and St Andrews, and with Loch Fitty (renowned for its brown trout) only walking distance from the hotel. The Halfway House is a good base for visitors to Fife.

Proprietor : W Lloyd

KIPPFORD

ANCHOR HOTEL
Kippford
Kirkcudbright
DG5 4LN
Tel: 055 662 205

Follow Solway coast road (A710) from Dalbeattie for 4 miles. Turn right for Kippford, 1 mile.

The Anchor Hotel is situated directly on the seafront, in picturesque Kippford on the Solway Coast, a village once known as the haunt of smugglers, and with lovely views over the estuary and the hills behind. With both its traditional wood panelled Anchor Bar and also the more modern lounge bar, the hotel is a popular spot for locals, holidaymakers and yachting fraternity alike. Facilities are also available for functions, catering for up to 120 people in a luxurious function suite. Interesting bar meals are available daily, with an extensive menu, catering for all tastes. Home-cooked specialities are featured each day and the menu offers everything from beefburgers to sirloin steaks and fish fingers to the Anchor 'Pints of Prawns'.

Tenant : Simon & Margaret Greig

KIRKCALDY

NICOL'S
8-10 Nicol Street
Kirkcaldy
KY1 1RP
Tel: 0592 268114

Once an old mill, Nicol's sits in the centre of Kirkcaldy and boasts a warm and comfortable interior in which to sit and relax away from the hustle and bustle of the town. The re-decoration has been carried out with taste and with attention to comfort, and has created an excellent atmosphere. Lunches are served in the lounge from 12 to 2.30 pm, high teas from 3 to 6 pm. Prices are very reasonable. In addition to the daytime menu, evening diners are catered for in the contiguous Mamma Mia's Italian restaurant which opens from 6 pm. Anything from pizzas and pastas to steaks is available from the open plan kitchen. Children are welcome and birthday celebrations are a speciality. The standard of the public areas is superb and alert management keeps them that way. Altogether this is an excellent inn, a credit to its owners and the trade in general.

Tennents Taverns

LANARK

WALLACE CAVE
11 Bloomgate
Lanark
ML11 9ET
Tel: 0555 3662

This is a modest but excellent little pub kept in first class condition and displaying a lot of care and taste in its interior fittings. The building is one of the oldest in Lanark and has connections with the great Scottish patriot, Sir William Wallace, whose wife was beheaded in the town by an invading English army. The pub boasts a fine selection of old malts, real ale and good beer. Bar snacks are available all day from 11 am to midnight and the pizzas are especially good. The lounge bar is cosy and well furnished and there is a small but excellent suite upstairs. An open fire from last century and lighting from copper stable lamps contribute to the atmosphere of the place.

Proprietor : James O'Connor

LATHERON

LATHERONWHEEL HOTEL
Latheron
Caithness
KW5 6DW
Tel: 05934 209

On A9, 1 mile south of (A895) Thurso turn-off.

Set back from the A9 at the north end of the village this is a typical small family run hotel. It is a popular stop for tourists going north or south on this main trunk road to and from John o'Groat's. Too many tourists feel that they have explored the north of Scotland if they get to Inverness and do not know what they are missing by failing to go further north. The Latheronwheel is known locally as 'The Blends' a probable reference to the days when whisky was blended on the premises. There is usually a welcoming coal fire in the lounge and a good choice of honest bar food during lunch and in the evening. The dining room is open for all meals including morning coffee and afternoon tea. There are four bedrooms.

Proprietors : Ronald & Eileen Sutherland

LESMAHAGOW

CRAIGNETHAN HOTEL

**69 Abbeygreen
Lesmahagow
Lanark
ML11 OEF
Tel: 0555 892333**

Turn off Junction 9 of M74.
In a rather lacklustre street, the Craignethan Hotel stands out prominently. Its white painted exterior and hanging flower baskets give it a cared for look. Lesmahagow is a conservation village and this is a very good village hotel with three separate bars and a snooker room. Its origins go back to the early 1600s. The interior has been refurbished with good taste and maintains the pleasing impression created by the outside appearance. The owner makes a point of welcoming everyone himself and this warm friendly attitude is carried through to an efficient staff. There is a good range of pub snacks and meals in both the lounge and public bar and a separate dining room for residents. An interesting and inviting village hotel.

Proprietor : Tom Renwick

LETHAM

FERNIE CASTLE HOTEL

**Letham
Cupar
Fife
KY7 7RU
Tel: 033 781 381**

On A914, 1 mile north of A91 intersection. Fernie Castle is a rugged old 16th century fortified house, now an elegant hotel. Its bars however are worthy of special mention. The Keep Bar is down some steps from the main entrance and is the original vaulted keep or stronghold with seven feet thick walls with arrow slits and a suit of armour apparently keeping guard at the entrance. Food is not served in this bar, but it is a refreshingly different place for a drink before lunch or dinner. The cocktail bar on the ground floor has a separate entrance from the garden and in the summer there are tables and chairs outside for the al fresco meal. This bar serves a satisfactory range of light snacks. This is a delightful location and a most suitable stopping-off point on the road to or from Dundee or Cupar.

Proprietors : Norman & Sheila Cinnamond

LEVEN

THE NEW CALEDONIAN HOTEL

**High Street
Leven
Fife
KY8 4NG
Tel: 0333 24101**

A smart modern building in the shopping precinct with a public car park nearby. The typical bistro lounge bar is on two levels with up to date decor and a profusion of artificial plants hanging from the ceiling. Clearly a popular spot with local business people and visitors. There is a very reasonable snack menu which on the day of our inspector's visit served excellent home-made soup and spaghetti bolognaise. Cheerful bar staff and waitresses give a good welcome. There are 16 comfortable

bedrooms with private bathrooms, TV and tea making facilities. An unusual type of pub but standards are high and food is good.
Proprietor: Thomas Herd

LEWIS

CALEDONIAN HOTEL

4-6 South Beach Street
Stornoway
Isle of Lewis
PA87 2XY
Tel: 0851 2411

Waterfront position on one of the main streets in Stornoway – adjacent to harbour and ferry terminal.

The first licensed establishment you reach on leaving the ferry, or the last before you board! Magnificent views of the bay from this hotel which has 10 en suite bedrooms and is close to shops. Ample car parking in the area. Locals frequent the bar in the evenings and it is popular with tourists travelling on the Ullapool ferry. Food is served 12 to 2.30 pm and in the evening, but because of local licensing laws children are not catered for in the bar. The Tropical Lounge Bar has an excellent reputation for bar lunches and has an unusual decor style for the remote Western Isles! There are tables and a marble top bar in a bright and airy terrace with hanging plants. Very high standard maintained by the caring and attentive staff.
Tennents Taverns

LIVINGSTON

COPPER TUN

Carmondean Centre
By Deans
Livingston
EH54 8PT
Tel: 0506 36767

Situated next to Safeway and Livingston North Railway Station.

This public house derives its name from the Copper Mash Tun suspended over the bar servery. It is a free standing pub with, externally, a clever use of dark wood and red facing brick. In its original use the striking central feature was capable of producing 4000 gallons of beer each brew and was in constant use until 1980 when it was restored to its present splendour. The Copper Tun also offers quality home-cooked food at lunchtime and in the evening. Nothing fancy but meeting public demand and the needs of its clientele. The smartly uniformed staff are courteous and cheerful and there is a high overall standard of cleanliness. There is also a family room, beer garden and a spacious conservatory which can be booked for functions and business seminars. Entertainment is also a regular feature at the Copper Tun.
Alloa Brewery

LOCHGOILHEAD

HERBS WINE BAR & BOUQUET GARNI RESTAURANT

Lochgoilhead
Argyll
PA24 8AJ
Tel: 030 13 206

The Bouquet Garni is well-known to everyone in the yachting fraternity and a great many others beside. This is a fun place, highly popular and run by a proprietor who knows his clientele outside in and doesn't miss a trick in the conduct of his business. The interior literally overflows with bric-a-brac. There is a small friendly bar laden with food on display and two aisles running off from it with booth seating. Upstairs is the more spacious Nico's Bar which is really the restaurant and comes into its own in the evenings. Mike Dimmer's fun menus with their phonetic spelling are worthy of a page in *Punch* magazine, but there is nonetheless some serious food of high standard both upstairs and down. This is very definitely a place not to be missed. Outrageously different, full of character and well worth a trip to Lochgoilhead. It is advisable to book in advance.
Proprietor: Mike Dimmer

LOCH LOMOND

ARDLUI HOTEL
**Loch Lomond
Dunbartonshire
G83 7EB
Tel: 030 14 243**

On A82 at the head of Loch Lomond. Beautifully situated amidst magnificent scenery on the shores at the head of Loch Lomond, this small countryside hotel offers comfort in a relaxed and friendly atmosphere. Originally built as a hunting lodge for the Colquhoun Clan Chiefs, extended in 1890 and again in 1905, it now has two bars, the Lomond and the lounge bar and two restaurants, both of which have superb views looking out over Loch Lomond. The Lomond Bar has original stone walls, oak beams and a large fireplace with log fire in winter. Both the Lomond and the lounge bar, which is luxuriously appointed, are open all day, all year round, and offer an extensive bar meals menu, which like the restaurants, feature fresh Loch Lomond salmon and sea trout (in season) and local venison. There are 11 bedrooms available (seven en suite) all with colour TV, radio alarms and tea/coffee making facilities. This is a good country inn with pleasant service and a value for money formula. It stands out like a beacon in an area remarkably short of decent pubs.
Proprietors: Mr & Mrs D B Squires

DUCK BAY HOTEL & MARINA
**Duck Bay
Loch Lomond
G83 8QZ
Tel: 0389 52789**

From Glasgow Airport on A82, 20 minutes. Glasgow city centre, 18 miles.
The Duck Bay Hotel stands on the banks of Loch Lomond just a mile from Balloch at the southern end of the loch. It enjoys magnificent views across the loch towards Ben Lomond. There is an adjacent Marina. A comfortable lounge, sundeck terraces and the Jetty Bar offer relaxation and suitable vantage points to watch the more energetic indulge in a variety of water sports. There is a fine restaurant serving lunch from 12 to 3 pm and candlelit dinner from 6 to 10 pm daily, but if you prefer something lighter, snacks are available in the lounge throughout the day until 8 pm. There are conference and function facilities, indeed something for almost everyone in this famous beauty spot.
Proprietor: R B Cawley

LOCHMABEN

BALCASTLE HOTEL
**High Street
Lochmaben
Dumfriesshire
DG11 1NG
Tel: 0387 810239**

A74 to Lockerbie then A709 to Dumfries. This is a large free standing sandstone building at the end of the main street with its lines softened by hanging flower baskets. It is adjacent to a nine hole golf course, and there is ample parking at front and rear. Balcastle is a pleasant, homely and relaxing place to which people return to follow their leisure pursuits in the neighbourhood. There is a large bar area offering a fairly extensive range of good home-made fare both at lunchtime and in the evening. All bedrooms have tea/coffee making facilities and TV. Most have private bathrooms or showers. Private salmon and trout fishing can be arranged for the enthusiast and there is coarse fishing at Lochmaben. Children and pets are welcome.
Proprietor: Mrs E G McGill

LONGFORGAN

THE LONGFORGAN HOTEL

Main Street
Longforgan
By Dundee
DD2 5EU
Tel: 082 622 386

A friendly well run rural pub with a beer garden, a car park and a play area for children. The bar is popular with locals, and anyone else who cares to drop in. A large comfortable lounge has doors on to the beer garden for long lazy summer days and evenings. There is an adequate menu choice. Portions are generous and good value for money. Quick service and friendly staff contribute to the pleasing impression this pub makes.

Proprietors : Mr & Mrs A G Wilson

LONGNIDDRY

THE LONGNIDDRY INN

Main Street
Longniddry
EH32 0NF
Tel: 0875 52401

A very attractive long and narrow pub converted from a row of cottages. The Longniddry Inn opened as a restaurant and bars in 1975 and maintained the atmosphere of a bygone age. It had for generations been inhabited by the Chernside family of blacksmiths who had established a fine reputation for workmanship in the area. Racehorses and local farm horses were shod in what is now known as the Forge Bar. The inn serves a good selection of home-cooked bar food running alongside a very competitively priced table d'hote menu and food is available all day. A well organised well run pub.

Alloa Brewery

MALLAIG

TIGH A CHLACHAIN

Mallaig
Inverness-shire
PH41
Tel: 0687 2124

Mallaig is a popular and convenient port to and from the Western Isles and frequent on the itinerary of those touring the west coast of Scotland. Tigh a Chlachain is a relatively simple pub but one which has earned a good reputation for the quality of its food. The menu is uncomplicated but entirely suitable for its clientele. The lounge bar has a rather dark appearance but the public bar with windows on the street is brighter. Our inspector was impressed with the polite friendly welcome and the neat clean appearance of the place. The management of this establishment is keen, and the high standard of food reflects this. Not a ritzy establishment but comfortable for a pleasing snack or social drink.

Proprietors : A & A Henderson

MARKINCH

TOWN HOUSE HOTEL

1 High Street
Markinch
Fife
KY7 6DQ
Tel: 0592 758459

Situated opposite railway station for Glenrothes.
Quality service, excellent food, served in pleasant surroundings. You'll find these essential ingredients in abundance at the Town House Hotel. The award winning Town House, a recently re-designed former coaching inn under the expert guidance of resident proprietors Harry and Lesley Bain, has built an enviable reputation for exciting cuisine and outstanding service. Conveniently situated close to major road and rail links, the Town House Hotel offers discerning diners a wide range of tastefully prepared traditional and exotic dishes. Lunchtimes or evenings, tempting meals are

served in the comfortable and relaxed surroundings of the Restaurant Lounge. The four beautifully furnished bedrooms are well equipped with colour TV, radio alarm, tea/coffee making facilities.
Proprietors : Mr & Mrs H Bain

MENSTRIE

BURNSIDE INN
1 Main Street West
Menstrie
FK19 8PR
Tel: 0259 61094

Situated between Bridge of Allan and Alva on A91.
Good housekeeping is apparent in this typical village hostelry – a handsome roadside building with ample car parking space at the rear. The cheerful public bar with adjoining 'snug' offers the full range of Alloa ales and lagers. An extensive home-cooked menu is served in the lounge bar every day and high teas are a speciality of the Burnsde Inn every Saturday, and are well worth trying. The service is warm and welcoming as you would expect in a well-run 'local'. The sort of place to stop at and not be disappointed.
Alloa Brewery
Tenant : H Thomson

MID CALDER

THE BLACK BULL
Market Street
Mid Calder
West Lothian
EH53 0AA
Tel: 0506 882170

At main crossroads of village.
The Black Bull must have presided over a lot of change in and around the Calders since it was established nearly 250 years ago. It is still a very dominant feature of the village. An old coaching inn, it has been altered and improved many times over the years yet there is a feeling of solid antiquity about it. There is a delightful cosy little public bar, attractively furnished, a large lounge bar furnished and carpeted with taste, and a charming dining room at the rear looking out over the garden. Bar meals in the lounge bar are really excellent value. The menu is wide enough to be interesting, food is piping hot and flavoursome and service is quick and efficient. Tables are cleared almost as soon as they are vacated. The dining room offers more formal meals of equally high standard and value. The whole establishment has a look of being cared for and first class staff do the same for the customers. Easy parking. Well worth visiting.
Welcome Inns

MOFFAT

BALMORAL HOTEL
High Street
Moffat
Dumfriesshire
DG10 9DL
Tel: 0683 20288

A fine example of an 18th century coaching inn located in the centre of the old spa town of Moffat which nestles in the picturesque Annan Valley. White painted shutters and colourful window boxes add to the external appearance. Moffat, frequent winner of the Most Beautiful Village in Scotland award, was a popular haunt of Rabbie Burns and the hotel, which was then known as the 'Old Spur Inn', was where he drank with the local schoolmaster, a Mr Clarke. A large selection of bar snacks during opening hours and more substantial meals in the dining room. There is good bedroom accommodation decorated and equipped to a high standard, several rooms with bathrooms en suite. This is an inn with a lot of character in an area with a lot of natural appeal. Certainly worth a diversion if your route does not take you directly through Moffat.
Proprietors : B Stokes & Family

MONIKIE

CRAIGTON COACH INN

**Craigton Road
Monikie
Angus
DD5 3QN
Tel: 082 623 223**

Turn left off main Dundee to Arbroath road (A92) about 7 miles outside Dundee (B961). Head for Monikie Country Park and follow signs to pub.

This charming country inn set just three miles off the main Dundee to Arbroath road adjacent to the popular Monikie Country Park, has low oak beamed ceilings complemented by a log fire and traditional mahogany bar and furniture. The menu is varied catering for all tastes including vegetarian dishes, and specialising in charcoal grilled fish and steaks. A children's menu is also available. The staff are welcoming and friendly and there are good facilities for children who are made most welcome here, in the family room adjacent to the lounge. Outside is a small beer garden and children's play area (open summer only). As well as traditional and cask conditioned ales there is a varied choice of malt whisky and low alcohol wines and lager. A really first class coaching inn which should appeal to almost everyone.

Proprietor : Irene Whitehead

MONTROSE

CORNER HOUSE HOTEL

**131 High Street
Montrose
Angus
DD10 8QN
Tel: 0674 73126**

Situated in the town centre on the south side of the steeple.

A well-established family business with many regular customers and a high reputation for good food and service. Sizzling Angus steaks and home-made sweets are specialities. Montrose is an ideal centre for the tourist. Angus glens, Royal Deeside, Glamis Castle and other historic castles and houses are in the area. Montrose is also a good centre for sportsmen with river and sea angling, wildfowling, shooting and bird watching on the tidal basin. There are many golf courses to suit all standards. The Corner House has 15 letting rooms most en suite. All rooms have TV, radio, telephone, tea/coffee makers and full central heating. The hotel is a privately owned free house and run by the resident proprietors Graham and Joyce Reid. This is a warm and comfortable place with well turned out staff offering efficient and pleasant service.

Proprietors : Graham & Joyce Reid

SALUTATION INN

**69-71 Bridge Street
Montrose
DD10 8AE
Tel: 0674 72832**

The Salutation is part of a row of cottages and has wisely kept the same external style. It has a well maintained beer garden to the rear which comes into its own in the summer. The interior is in traditional Scottish pub style with separate lounge and bar areas. There are several nice touches such as fresh flowers and plants on the lounge bar and there is a distinctly pleasant welcoming atmosphere. Lunches are served in the lounge bar and bar snacks are available at all other opening times. The menu is limited but well priced and the quality is good. The staff are excellent, immediately welcoming and friendly and efficient. This is an excellent example of the traditional pub in Scotland, in its design, interior fittings and furnishings. A very pleasant pub, well run and friendly and difficult to fault in any category.

Proprietor : William Moir

MUSSELBURGH

WOODSIDE HOTEL
30 Linkfield Road
Musselburgh
EH21 7LL
Tel: 031 665 2155

Situated on the main road through Musselburgh.

A very imposing three storey building overlooking the racecourse on the main road through Musselburgh just outside Edinburgh. It has recently been upgraded to a high standard and the premises comprise a comfortable cocktail bar, restaurant and two function rooms which have established an excellent reputation over the years especially for weddings. An extensive lunch menu is available every day between 12 and 2 pm with dinner being served in the evenings from 6.30 to 9.30 pm. There are eleven letting bedrooms with private facilities, all of which have been tastefully decorated and offer a high degree of comfort. There is a welcoming feel about this place, much attention to detail, and it is clear that high standards prevail throughout.

Alloa Brewery
Tenant : Alan C Russell

NAIRN

COVENANTERS INN
Auldearn
By Nairn
Inverness-shire
IV12 5TG
Tel: 0667 52456

Just off A86, 2 miles east of Nairn.

This is a clever conversion of an old mill and brewhouse dating from the Battle of Auldearn in 1645. There is dark oak furniture and low beams, and a warm welcome from the log fire in the winter. In the summer months there is an attractive patio in which to enjoy a leisurely drink. The inn has a fine reputation for its local seafood and game which are served all day in the summer months. There are eight en suite bedrooms with all facilities and an attractive restaurant with attached conservatory. Within easy reach are championship golf courses, excellent fishing, castles and many beautiful beaches.

Proprietors : Colin & Ros Thompson

NIGG

THE GORDON HOTEL
Wellington Road
Nigg
Aberdeen
AB1 4JT
Tel: 0224 873012

On the southern outskirts of Aberdeen. Approaching from the south take the 'Harbour' road, which passes the hotel.

The Gordon Grill Room which is open for lunch and dinner 12 to 2.30 pm and 6.30 to 9.30 pm seven days a week is backed up by a traditional bar food operation, which provides for both tourist and visitors, and is a popular lunchtime venue for local businessmen to unwind and enjoy inexpensive quality food, served promptly in pleasant surroundings. The Gordon Hotel has some 26 rooms, most of them with private facilities which provide excellent quality budget cost accommodation.

Alloa Brewery

NORTH QUEENSFERRY

FERRY BRIDGE HOTEL
1 Main Street
North Queensferry
Fife
KY11 1JQ
Tel: 0383 416292

With the famous Forth Railway Bridge towering above it, North Queensferry seems like a village in miniature. Once the Fife base of the ferry over the Forth, this village is a haven of peace since the bustle of the traffic takes its journey across the Forth Road Bridge. The streets are narrow and wind round the contours of the land on the waters edge. The Ferry Bridge Hotel is on

cont. p. 81

the main street of North Queensferry. It has a lounge bar where you immediately feel as comfortable as if you were in your own sitting room. The glow of the fire, the comfortable furnishings and pleasant decor combine with the bric-a-brac and paraphernalia to create a warm and homely atmosphere. Bar meals are available through the archway to the adjoining room. A cosy relaxing place to unwind, and for an enjoyable informal meal.

NORTH KESSOCK

NORTH KESSOCK HOTEL

Main Street
North Kessock
Ross & Cromarty
IV1 1XM
Tel: 0463 73 208

On A9, 1 mile north of Kessock Bridge, near Inverness.
Colonial style family run village hotel overlooking the Beauly Firth where dolphins play most days. Delightful patio and garden area to enjoy the delicious bar lunches and suppers in the summer days and evenings. Open all year round. All bedrooms offer private facilities at reasonable tariff. Inverness and Loch Ness within minutes. Ideally situated for visitors exploring the north and north-west Scotland. Golf and fishing close by.
Proprietors: Mr & Mrs D MacLachlan

OBAN

AULAY'S BAR

8 Airds Place
Oban
Argyll
Tel: 0631 62596

A favourite with both locals and visitors alike. The bar was recently refurbished and highly commended in the 1988 Guinness Design Award. The bar was also featured on Scottish radio as being unique because the walls are totally covered with pictures of boats both old and new but all have sailed in local waters. A collection worth seeing! A bar of character where you can get a friendly welcome in a relaxed atmosphere. A bar that cares.
Proprietor: Aulay Dunn

THE BARN BAR

Cologin
Lerags, By Oban
Argyll
PA34 4SE
Tel: 0631 64501

One mile off A816 when 2 miles south of Oban.
This is a small country pub, with a warm friendly atmosphere, set on an old farm beside the drove road from the islands to the lowlands. Good home-made food at sensible prices is served in the lounge bar all day and throughout the evenings. There are tables set outside with wonderful views of the countryside, where you may like to feed the ducks, hens and Peter the donkey. A great place for kids of all ages. Entertainment is held three nights weekly during the high season with a ceilidh/barbecue on Thursday evenings, complete with piper and Highland dancer. Tuesday evening is live accordion music, with folk, country and western, and rock'n'roll on Saturdays. There are 18 timber bungalows which sleep from two to six persons available for self-catering or bed and breakfast. This is a clean, cheerful and welcoming family pub.
Proprietor: Henry Woodman

OLD KILPATRICK

TELSTAR PUBLIC HOUSE & RESTAURANT

316 Dumbarton Road
Old Kilpatrick
Glasgow
G60 5JH
Tel: 0389 72938

A82, 8 miles east of Loch Lomond and 9 miles from Glasgow city centre.
Situated in the picturesque village of Old Kilpatrick by the banks of the Clyde and close to the Erskine Bridge. This is a recently

refurbished modern pub with many up market features but holding its prices at the level of the average 'local'. The proprietor is usually on the spot to ensure standards of service and the principles of good, home-cooked food are being maintained. The menu is extensive and has been prepared thoughtfully and not just thrown together. The restaurant is pleasant and comfortable and the bar exudes a good pub atmosphere. Food is available from lunch throughout the day. A very good value for money four course dinner with an Italian theme is served Monday to Friday. There are also good steaks and salmon on the a la carte menu. This is a pub that tries hard to maintain high standards and seemingly satisfies an extensive clientele.

Proprietor : William Gray

ONICH

LOCH LEVEN HOTEL

Onich
Nr Fort William
PH33 6SA
Tel: 08553 236

By the old ferry slipway on the north side of Ballachulish Bridge.

A family run 17th century former coaching inn which sits well in its tidy grounds in this very beautiful area of the west. The proprietors welcome families and indeed make special provision for them. In-house films are shown during the season and there is a leisure centre with indoor bowling and snooker. The lounge bar serves straightforward wholesome food at moderate prices from 12 to 2 pm and between 6 and 9 pm. There is a more extensive a la carte menu in the dining room utilising fresh local produce wherever possible. Plenty of sporting and recreational facilities nearby. Comfortable accommodation with some rooms having en suite bathrooms.

Proprietors : Messrs Young & McArthur

THE LODGE ON THE LOCH

Creag Dhu
Onich,
Nr Fort William
Inverness-shire
PH33 6RY
Tel: 08553 237/238

On the main A82, 10 miles south of Fort William – 1 mile before the Ballachulish Bridge.

Superbly set above Loch Linnhe, this warm and welcoming hotel commands a spectacular panorama of mountain and loch. The Lodge on the Loch has long had a reputation for its elegance and special charm that have set it apart from other four crown hotels. You can discover this for yourself – call in at lunchtime for a refreshingly original (and inexpensive) bar lunch. Or even better, settle back over dinner in the restaurant and watch the sun set over the waters, but stay overnight if you can. The bedrooms are comfortable and almost all have private facilities. The hotel is usually open from March to October and over Christmas and New Year.

Proprietors : The Young Family

ORMISTON

THE MOFFAT ARMS

The Wynd
Ormiston
East Lothian
Tel: 0875 610538

Off A1 by Tranent, 2 miles.

There is nothing pretentious about the Moffat Arms but it is a comfortable and charming village inn, well maintained and in good condition. Ormiston is a conservation area, and well worth a visit for that reason. It is the birthplace of Robert Moffat who was a missionary and probably the first white man in Rhodesia. He was also father-in-law to another famous Scottish explorer and missionary, David Livingstone. Bar snacks which are served at lunchtime and in the evening are imaginative and interesting.

Lunches are available Fridays, Saturdays and Sundays and evening meals Friday and Saturday (Sunday bookings pm). Roy, June and Lucy Baines run the Moffat Arms to a high standard and make guests feel welcome.

Proprietors : Roy & June Baines

PAISLEY

BRABLOCH HOTEL
**62 Renfrew Road
Paisley PA3 4RD
Tel: 041 889 5577**

On the main Renfrew-Paisley road, c.½ mile south of exit 27 of M8 which is 1 mile east of Glasgow Airport.

The Brabloch Hotel is an imposing mansion house, almost 200 years old, with later additions, set in four acres of grass and trees, within walking distance of Paisley town centre with all its old religious and historical associations. Patricia and Lewis Grant have built up a fine reputation for functions in the several function suites available in this hotel but of course there is also a good selection of bar snacks at lunchtime and until 10 pm in the evening. There is the Gallery Restaurant for the more leisurely meal. Staff are cheerful, service is excellent, and the place is well-maintained inside and out. There are 46 bedrooms with all modern facilities.

Proprietors : Mr & Mrs Lewis Grant

HAMILTON'S
**4 Calside
Paisley
PA2 6DA
Tel: 041 887 2217**

This is a simple straightforward traditional pub catering primarily for the local population. It is on a main road and unfortunately has no car park but vehicles can usually find a parking place nearby. It has a well furnished attractive lounge bar and a small family room completely separate from the bar where children can join in family groups. The bar menu is available from 12 to 2 pm and from 5 to 9 pm. Food is unpretentious but of good standard and is geared to the requirement of the clientele. The premises are maintained in excellent condition with everything neat and tidy throughout. Service is speedy from a cheerful caring staff. Hamilton's makes no claim to be an up-market ritzy pub. It is what it is, and what it does it does well and it sets good standards.

Proprietor : A J Cole-Hamilton

HARVIES
**86 Glasgow Road
Paisley
PA1 3LY
Tel: 041 889 0911**

Harvies is a very popular rendezvous particularly with business and professional people and it is not difficult to understand why. Superb decor and first class food have much to do with it but are not the only factors. This is a pub that has set out to establish and maintain high standards and it has succeeded. Considering the quality of the place, prices are very reasonable and the service is quite excellent. The staff always find time for a welcoming smile and a word or two with everyone. There is live entertainment seven nights a week. This is a top category establishment reflecting credit on the Stakis Organisation and on its management.

Proprietor : Stakis plc

LORD LOUNSDALE
**17 Lounsdale Road
Paisley
Tel: 041 889 6263**

This is a superb pub. The single storey building is very attractive from the outside and even more so when you get inside. There are cosy bars and a restaurant warmed by a large open fire. Lots of bric-a-brac give atmosphere to the place. Speciality dishes are prepared daily by the chefs and as much local produce as possible is used. Very efficient waiting staff provide first class service. Perhaps a measure of the popularity of the Lord Lounsdale is the fact that the car park takes over 100 vehicles. This is clearly a good pub with a lot of appeal and one that is unlikely to disappoint.

Tennents Taverns

PENICUIK

THE OLD HOWGATE INN

Wester Howgate
Nr Penicuik
EH26 8QB
Tel: 0968 74244

This is a former coaching inn, the first stop for the Edinburgh to Dumfries coach. It is a very old cottage and attractive style building and the bar area is tiny with a huge fireplace. Although the main feature of the inn is the restaurant, there is also a limited bar menu specialising in open sandwiches. The restaurant menu is more extensive and offers excellent and good value food. A popular venue for a meal out. Service in the bar is attentive and prompt and the atmosphere is certainly cosy. The Howgate is held in high affection by Edinburghers and is well-known to several generations of them. The atmosphere is different and the drive out to it delightful.

Proprietor: Steven Arthur

PERTH

ALMONDBANK INN

Almondbank
By Perth
PH1 3NJ
Tel: 0738 83 242

Half mile off A85 Crieff road, 4 miles from Perth.
Situated on the banks of the River Almond within an idyllic setting this is an excellent place to enjoy a good eating experience. There is an extensive lunch menu seven days 12 to 2.45 pm. A superb supper menu from 5 pm (Sunday to Thursday) or the renowed 'Candlelit Dinner' Friday/Saturday evening. All at very affordable prices, all served in an attractive and tastefully decorated restaurant and lounge. Complemented with an excellent selection of beers, wines and spirits and also a range of non-alcoholic wines and soft drinks, and for those hot summer days a lovely beer garden overlooking the River Almond. See the Flowerpot Fantasy Garden.

Proprietors: Charles & Elizabeth Lindsay

SILVER BROOM

Canal Street
Perth
Tel: 0738 25945

The corner site of the Silver Broom at Canal Street and Scott Street is just a few minutes walk from the town centre. It has a public bar on the ground floor with a pool table and TV which seems to be primarily patronised by the men, while upstairs is an attractive and interesting lounge catering for a mixed clientele. Food in the lounge bar is of good quality and very good value – indeed the bar lunch has been featured in the *Sunday Post*. The staff are friendly, polite and efficient even at a busy lunchtime. This pub is popular, and its pleasant relaxed atmosphere, combined with the standard to which it is maintained attract custom from all directions. Most people will find it a pleasant experience.

Proprietor: R P Deveaux

WINDSOR BAR

38 St John Street
Perth
PH1 5SP
Tel: 0738 23969

A substantial large fronted inn in the main shopping area with a well maintained look about it. It lacks a car park but there are ticket machine parking facilities nearby. The large lounge bar is of pleasing decor with a mixture of buffet and chair seating and unobtrusive background music. The menu sticks to the popular demand items and is fairly restricted but of good quality. The bar staff are very pleasant and helpful. The popularity of this establishment is a tribute to its standards. It knows its market and caters well for it, providing a comfortable ambience for a relaxed meal or social drink.

Welcome Inns

PLOCKTON

PLOCKTON HOTEL
41 Harbour Street
Plockton
Wester Ross
IV52 8TN
Tel: 059 984 274

Nestling in the waterside village of Plockton, with its beautiful yacht anchorage and majestic scenery, the Plockton Hotel has chosen its site well. The interior has a nautical flavour to it, but not aggressively so and it is a warm friendly pub with a quiet relaxed air to it. There is a first class selection of bar foods and children are well catered for. If you get the opportunity do try the fresh Plockton prawns in their shells with an accompanying dip. Prices are very modest. This is a delightful place at which to stop off when touring the west coast. You will not want to hurry away. Take an extra film with you. No one will believe the tropical palm trees!

Proprietors : Alasdair & Lynn Bruce

POOL O' MUCKHART

THE INN AT MUCKHART
Pool o' Muckhart
By Dollar
Clackmannanshire
Tel: 025981 324

A91 Stirling to St Andrews road 3 miles east of Dollar.
In the middle of Pool o' Muckhart, which has won Scotland's Best Kept Village Award on a number of occasions, this 19th century inn nestles at the foot of the Ochil Hills. The original timber beamed ceiling and the open log fire provide an ambience that both locals and visitors enjoy. The interior is warm and comfortable with polished mahogany tables and a very attentive and welcoming staff. Excellent value lunches and suppers are served daily in the traditionally furnished inn, which has a small beer garden and also has ample parking facilities. There is a two bedroomed fully furnished cottage adjoining the inn which is let for minimum periods of four days. "Overseas visitors would love it" claimed our inspector. So too do locals and itinerant Britons.

Proprietors : Mr & Mrs Shiels

PORTPATRICK

CROWN HOTEL
North Crescent
Portpatrick
DG9 8SX
Tel: 077681 409

Adjacent to harbour on sea front.
The interior of this charming old inn is in surprising and marked contrast to the austere exterior. Warm and welcoming with oak beams, dark wood furniture and a cheery fire in the cold weather. It stands only a few yards from the water's edge facing across the harbour to the Irish Channel. The staff takes pride in the hotel's well established and well merited reputation for good food. Somewhat naturally there is an emphasis on seafood but there is a good range of alternative dishes available also. There is a spacious dining room and conservatory. Bar meals are available at lunchtime and in the evenings. Bedrooms are tastefully furnished and have private bathrooms, colour TVs, tea making facilities etc.

Proprietor : B Wilson

PRESTWICK

THE RED LION INN & RESTAURANT
9 The Cross
Prestwick
KA9 1AG
Tel: 0292 70703

A famous old hostelry where in 1851 it was decided to form a golf club in Prestwick. Four years later the first ever Open Golf Championship was held in Prestwick. It is situated at the west end of the main street, five minutes drive from the shore and

Prestwick Airport. Currently a newly refurbished inn with a 70 seater steak based restaurant. The bar is attractive in an 'old oak' style with tables to match and a good feeling of spaciousness. The bar food is conventional while the restaurant has a wide choice of typical steakhouse fare at standard prices. Families are made welcome and a children's menu is featured. There is a large car park at rear. This is a solid dependable pub converted to a modern steakhouse which will appeal to visitors and will not let the side down.
Welcome Inns

RHU

THE ARDENCAPLE HOTEL
Shore Road
Rhu GA8 8LA
Tel: 0436 820 200

Travel north on A814 from Helensburgh for 1 mile. Hotel is situated on lochside, just before Rhu village.

An 18th century coaching inn, comprising 14 letting bedrooms, all recently refurbished to a high standard, a saloon bar frequented by submariners from the local Faslane Base, an attractive lounge bar with conservatory off, and a quaint restaurant looking out over the Gareloch. Bar food is served daily from noon till late at night all through the day and the restaurant is open each evening serving quality Scottish fare at prices to suit most pockets.
Alloa Brewery

ROSLIN

YE OLDE ORIGINAL ROSLIN INN
4 Main Street
Roslin
Midlothian EH25 9LE
Tel: 031 440 2514/2384

Roslin is a nice little village just a few miles out from Edinburgh, noted for the famous Rosslyn Chapel. Local legend has it that the Holy Grail is built into the walls of the Chapel – an architecturally delightful building. The hotel is a very attractive two storey building at the end of the main street in the village. Exposed stone walls and alcove type seating within the small lounge bar make for an intimate and cosy atmosphere. Bar meals are served in the lounge. Good portions of basic home-cooked wholesome dishes. The standard of service is very high and there is good attention to detail in the maintenance of the public areas. Overall well worth a visit. Rosslyn Chapel will always go on drawing lots of visitors to it and the old Roslin Inn makes a delightful place for a meal or a pleasant and relaxing drink with friends.
Proprietor: The Harris Family

ROSYTH

CLEO'S
170 Queensferry Road
Rosyth KY11 2JF
Tel: 0383 413657

On main road in Rosyth.
Guesses are that this up-market and stylish lounge bar takes its name from the main feature there – a full size bust of Cleopatra! Both the restaurant and lounge bar are fitted out with bamboo furniture. The front portion of the building is like a conservatory restaurant with large plants against the windows and swagged curtains. Lunch is served in both lounge bar and restaurant daily, but supper and dinner available Thursday to Saturday, only with disco. The

public areas are of a good standard, but perhaps the spotlights and sparkling coloured balls are out of place except on disco nights. However a very good pleasant staff provide the attentive service.
Tennents Taverns

RUTHERGLEN

BANK INN
159 King Street
Rutherglen G73 1BX
Tel: 041 647 6447

A well appointed modern public bar and lounge, just behind the main shopping street and with adequate car parking facilities. It has a cheerful friendly air to it and all age groups would feel welcome. There is a good menu and every effort is made to use fresh produce and present quality food. Lunch meals are available at the usual time of midday to 3 pm Monday to Saturday and snacks are available throughout the day from noon till 11 pm. The premises are well kept, constant attention being given to clearing tables, replacing ashtrays etc, and the staff are thoroughly pleasant and helpful. A good pub with a very good atmosphere.
Alloa Brewery

ST JOHNS TOWN OF DALRY

LOCHINVAR HOTEL
3 Main Street
St Johns Town of Dalry
Kirkcudbrightshire DG7 3UP
Tel: 064 43 210

A slate and sandstone building with attractive creepers on the walls, and standing right on the main Ayr-Castle Douglas road. The interior has been tastefully decorated with a concentration on the comfort of guests and a particular emphasis on good food. Meals are available throughout the day. Bar meals from 11 am until near midnight, and there are afternoon teas and high teas and a very extensive menu in the lovely dining room from 7 pm till late. Many of the bedrooms have private bathrooms and are well equipped. This is really a very comfortable wayside inn, well worth a stop en route. Emphasis is on quality and that is a formula which usually succeeds.
Proprietors: Mr & Mrs P J Bryant

SANQUHAR

NITHSDALE HOTEL
High Street
Sanquhar DG4 6DJ
Tel: 0659 50506

Most people speeding along the A74 are totally oblivious to the really delightful country to the west of them. Upper Nithsdale in the heart of Dumfriesshire is an area not to be missed and Sanquhar on the A76 is the logical stopping place – particularly for anglers. The Nithsdale is a pleasant surprise in such a small town. James Anderson the proprietor has invested time and thought to produce a delightful bar and dining room. You can enjoy bar meals from quite an extensive menu in the cocktail bar or eat a la carte to a high standard in the dining room. There are half a dozen comfortable bedrooms with colour TV and the usual tea making facilities. If you are not an angler there is quite a lot to see in the near neighbourhood – the lead mining museum at Wanlockhead (the highest village in Scotland) or Drumlanrig Castle, home of the Duke of Buccleuch. Of course in an area of natural beauty there is hill walking and bird watching.
Proprietor: James Anderson

SKYE

SKEABOST HOUSE HOTEL
Skeabost Bridge
Isle of Skye IV51 9NP
Tel: 047 032 202

Our inspector could scarcely find enough superlatives to incorporate in his report on Skeabost. "Absolutely superb. Very, very comfortable. Would recommend it to anyone" is enough to give the flavour of the impression it created on him. But then

Skeabost is a rather special place. There are three lounges, a cocktail bar and an enthusiastic young staff anxious to do all they can to maintain the high reputation of the place. Food and bedrooms are equally impressive. If you are on Skye this is one not to be missed. If you are on the mainland it is worth going to the island.

Proprietors: Messrs McNab, Stuart & McNab

SOUTH QUEENSFERRY

THE HAWES INN

Newhalls Road
South Queensferry
EH30 9TA
Tel: 031 331 1990

The Hawes Inn, South Queensferry, has a magnificent site overlooking the graceful lines of the Forth Road Bridge, and the world famous cantilever Forth Railway Bridge opened in March 1890. The inn comprises a lounge bar and public bar serving good bar food, a tasteful a la carte restaurant offers food of a very high standard and features a selection of Scottish dishes to tempt the palate. You can stay overnight at the inn in one of its quaint bedrooms, one of which was occupied by Robert Louis Stevenson who was to immortalise the Hawes Inn in his book *Kidnapped*. This is a place steeped in history, well worth a visit if only for a drink and a meal in this wonderful setting. But stay if you can. Lots of parking behind the inn. Special arrangements are made for parties.

Alloa Brewery

STENHOUSEMUIR

THE DYKES

Mount Gerald
Stenhousemuir
By Larbert FK5 4DY
Tel: 03245 58805

An excellent external appearance instantly attracts. The place looks inviting and well-maintained as are the gardens and car park. The atmosphere inside is warm and friendly,

with family clientele, very comfortable seating and pleasant surroundings. The staff seem eager to live up to the standards of the establishment and, of course, do much to make those standards. Good bar food with a bias to home-cooking is available all day long and is remarkably inexpensive. This is a splendid type of country pub, reflecting good management, style and standards.

Welcome Inns

STIRLING

THE BIRDS AND THE BEES

Easter Cornton Road
Causewayhead
Stirling FK9 5PB
Tel: 0786 73663

Converted old farm buildings may have something to do with the unusual name of this place. Whether they have or not is immaterial. This is a delightful conversion from agricultural use, with old farm implements contributing to the overall appearance. Inside, the rustic simplicity creates a splendid atmosphere. Bar food is available at lunchtime Monday to Thursday and from noon till 10 pm, Fridays and Saturdays. There is a separate dining room and a large function suite. In the past it has has been voted best pub in Scotland. It continues to be good. Altogether a very different, intriguing hostelry somewhat off the beaten track but well worth finding.

Proprietor: R Henderson

WHISKY FROM THE OLD SCHOOL
TEACHER'S
HIGHLAND CREAM
Perfection of Old
SCOTCH WHISKY
Wm Teacher & Sons Ltd
GLASGOW SCOTLAND
Distilled, Blended & Bottled in Scotland
75cl e
40% vol

OLDE ENGLISH, BABYCHAM, COPPERHEAD
- BRAND LEADERS - TRENDSETTERS - PROFIT MAKERS -

Gaymer's Olde English Cyder

- Highest rate of sale among major brands on draught.
- Now the fastest-growing established cyder brand on draught.
- Unique filtering process not used by our competitors.

THE definitive, original strong cyder.

- Brings a sparkle to all occasions - all seasons.
- Chosen by over 6 million women each year.
- Dazzling, durable P.O.S. planned for 1989.
- Heavyweight media spend this year, including TV.

Babycham

Nothing - but NOTHING sparkles like a Babycham.

Copperhead Cider

- 1st major new draught cider in 20 years - 80% awareness levels in advertised regions.
- Pressed, fermented & filtered for a sharper edge and harder body.
- Dynamic new advertising campaign directed at bringing new consumers into the market.

Cider made the hard way.

Showerings Ltd - Kilver Street - Shepton Mallet - Somerset - BA4 5ND.

THERE'S A

WELCOME

MAT

IN

EVERY

ALLOA PUB.

Our attention to quality means we offer nothing but the best. An impressive range of beers and lagers. A wide choice of soft drinks and low alcohol beers. And a tempting selection of good food. With something to suit all tastes. We look forward to welcoming you to an Alloa pub soon.

ALLOA

SPARKLE. DON'T FIZZ.

ARTHUR BELL DISTILLERS
THE UK'S LARGEST SPIRITS COMPANY

REFLECTING QUALITY AND PROFIT

For further information or to place an order please contact Arthur Bell Distillers, Cherrybank, Perth, Scotland PH2 0NG. Telephone: 0345 444111

PURE GENIUS

THE FAMOUS GROUSE
COUNTRY OF ORIGIN–SCOTLAND NOTED FOR
ITS CHARACTER AND DISTINGUISHED APPEARANCE

Quality in an age of change.

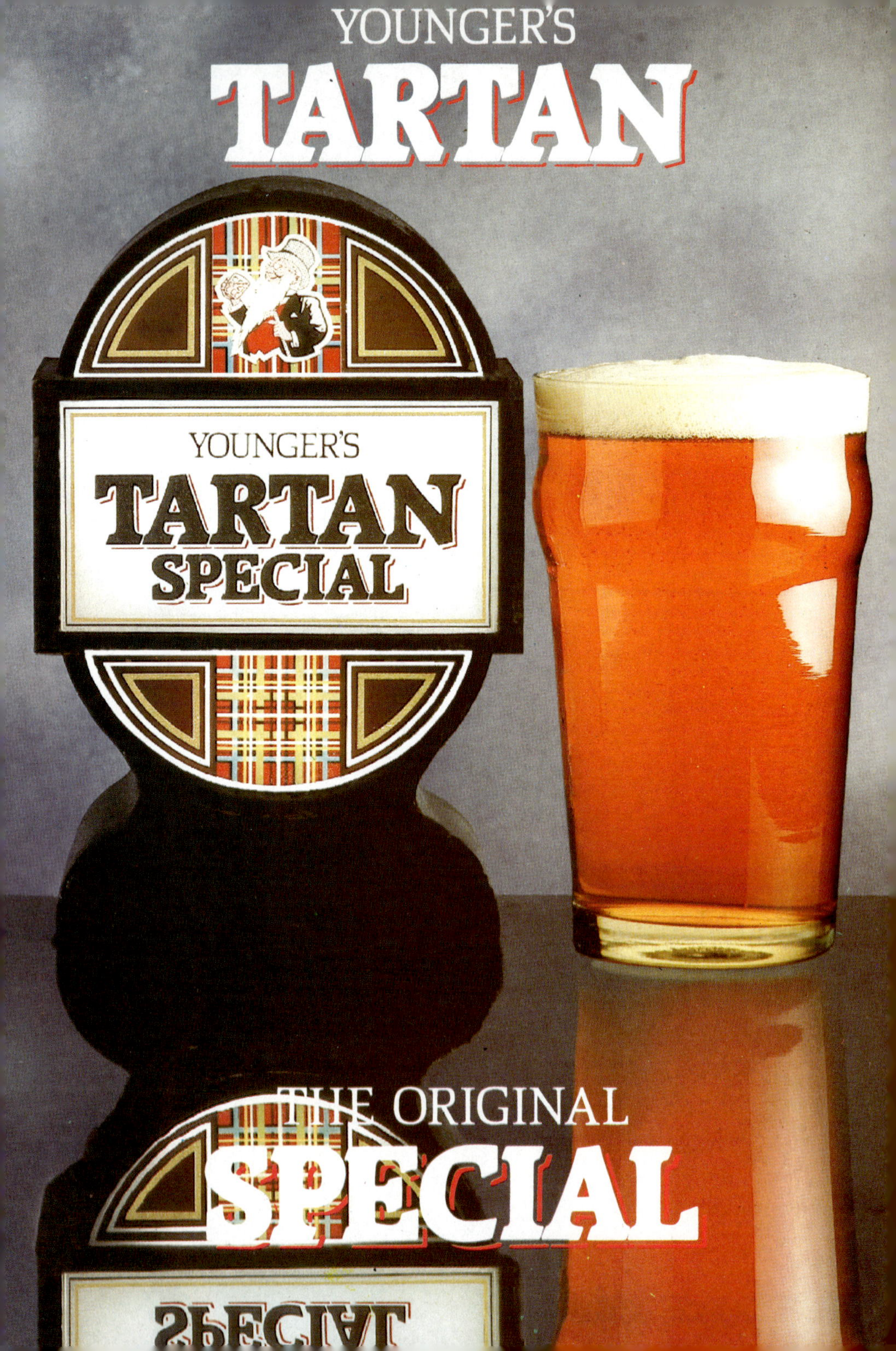
YOUNGER'S
TARTAN
YOUNGER'S
TARTAN
SPECIAL
THE ORIGINAL
SPECIAL

THE CASTLE HOTEL
**Castle Wynd
Stirling FK8 1EG
Tel: 0786 72290/75621**

Just below the Esplanade of Stirling Castle. This old stone building has in its long history been an ammunition store and a grammar school. Today it is a hotel of character and also a good resting place on the route up to the castle or a reviver on the return trip! You enter through a gateway in the old stone exterior, which leads you to the lounge bar, hotel reception and the small beer garden set within the walls. The lounge bar had a good fire burning on the night of our inspector's visit and was warmly lit. The Jacobean decor – tapestried seating and heavy wooden tables – created an atmosphere of times long gone by, steeped in the history of the period. Very pleasant staff – good hospitality. Food available in lounge bar and in the separate dining room 12 to 9.30 pm. Well worth a visit.

Proprietor: T F Catterson

COURTYARD
**Rock Terrace
Backwalk
Stirling
Tel: 0786 72651**

The Courtyard is steeped in history. It is built into the old town wall which surrounded Stirling in mediaeval times. Locals know it well but it is not too easy to find so if you are a visitor do ask for instructions. It would be a pity to miss it. There is an inviting entrance and the interior is very trendy and well looked after. It has a lounge bar, restaurant and bistro. Patisserie is served from 9 am each day with lunch from 12 noon through the afternoon. Evening meals are available till 10.30 pm. The menu is quite extensive, mainly pasta type dishes, and a blackboard highlights special items. There is a beer garden and a function suite. Children are welcomed. The Courtyard is run to a very high standard and this is obvious in the degree of maintenance in the public areas.

Proprietor: Castle Leisure Group

STONEHAVEN

MARINE HOTEL
**9-10 Shorehead
Stonehaven
Kincardineshire AB3 2JY
Tel: 0569 62155**

Off A94 follow signs for the harbour.
A family run hotel set on the picturesque Stonehaven harbour providing some pleasant views of harbour activity. Somewhat naturally the interior features a fishing theme with brass ornaments and storm lamps. There is a fairly extensive menu with generous portions and an emphasis on seafood and home-cooking. Food presentation is good. Bar lunches are served from 12 to 2 pm and from 5 to 10 pm. There is a separate dining room for more formal eating. The staff dress casually but are cheerful and welcoming. There are eight bedrooms all with a sea view, and families are welcome.

Proprietors: Phil & Jackie Duncan

STONEHOUSE

CROSS KEYS INN
**7 Queen Street
Stonehouse
Lanarkshire ML9 3EE
Tel: 0698 791221**

A free standing pub with relatively easy parking outside the premises. The proprietor, George Golder, has put a lot into modernising the bar and lounge bar of this century old building. It has been tastefully furnished and is maintained to a very high standard. There is a nice homely atmosphere to it and an aura of friendliness from the owner and his staff. Fresh produce is used wherever possible. The menu is limited but well balanced and service is excellent. Lunches are served from noon till 3 pm daily and evening meals are available Friday, Saturday and Sunday. Children are made welcome. Altogether this is a really first class pub, well worth a visit for a drink or a meal.

Proprietor: George C Golder

STONEYWOOD

THE RUNWAY INN
275 Stoneywood Road
Stoneywood
Aberdeen AB2 9RR
Tel: 0224 712705

The Runway Inn – as its name suggests – has aviation as its theme. It is a free standing building on the Aberdeen-Old Meldrum road in the vicinity of the airport. The dark panelled walls, hung with pictures of aircraft, and the low ceiling combine to create a cosy atmosphere. It has a regular busy lunchtime trade, with a mainly business clientele. Bar meals are served in the lounge and the public bar. There is a good choice of food, keenly priced, both at lunch and in the evening. Snacks are available all afternoon. The Runway Inn is a popular place and provides good value for money.
Proprietor: David Bisset

SYMINGTON

WHEATSHEAF INN
Main Street
Symington
Ayrshire
Tel: 0563 830 307

Appropriately rural in appearance the Wheatsheaf is an attractive single storey building on a corner site with a well maintained car park and a small beer garden. It has been furnished in country style decor and this has been done well. There is an extensive menu and a separate dining room. Food is prepared with care and presented with imagination and has earned the Wheatsheaf a well deserved reputation for quality. This is a place where staff and customers all seem cheerful and welcoming and obviously feel comfortable in the homely atmosphere of the place. A good track record has been established and seems likely to be maintained and even improved.
Belhaven Brewery
Tenant: R Armour & H Thompson

TARBERT

BARMORE FARM
Barmore
Tarbert
Argyll PA29 6YJ
Tel: 08802 222

2 miles north of Tarbert.
Attractive and charmingly restored Listed farm steading offering bar and restaurant, as well as self-catering cottages. There is a small but adequate bar with its own dining area where seafood is a speciality and the prices are reasonable. In addition there is a separate dining room. Bar open for bar lunches and suppers, though closed afternoons and Monday and Tuesday in the spring. Very friendly and professional service. Barmore Farm is a member of the Taste of Scotland Scheme – which says much for its standards.
Proprietors: Graeme & Elizabeth Scott

THORNHILL

GEORGE HOTEL
103-106 Drumlanrig Street
Thornhill
Dumfriesshire DG3 5LU
Tel: 0848 30326

On A76, 14 miles north of Dumfries.
The George is a nice old coaching inn in picturesque Nithsdale, a district of Scotland with lots of leisure pursuits but too often bypassed by frantic tourists rushing north or south. It is a family run hotel recently refurbished, and though small it is friendly and welcoming. A fairly extensive bar meal menu is served seven days a week and a more extensive supper menu is available and was clearly very popular at the time of our inspector's visit. Prices are reasonable. Most bedrooms are en suite and have TV, tea making facilities and telephone.
Proprietor: Robert Saville

THURSO

GROVE LOUNGE
Grove Lane
Thurso KW14
Tel: 0847 64588

Thurso – town centre between Co-op and Presto shops.
In this most northerly town of the Scottish mainland there is much history to be absorbed and lots of interesting things to do. The Grove Lounge has all the comfort and atmosphere of a lounge bar. Its walls are adorned with fossils from local quarries and the sturdy fireplace was built by a local tradesman. The Grove has a daily changing lunchtime menu while an extensive standard menu is available all day long. Portions are generous and well presented and there is an emphasis on local fare. There is live country music on many evenings. This is an attractive establishment with a good reputation locally. It is part of a large leisure complex which also has a licensed restaurant.
Proprietor: L R MacLean

PENTLAND HOTEL
Princes Street
Thurso
Caithness KW14 7AA
Tel: 0847 63202

A comfortable solid hotel of Victorian construction, well furnished throughout and with a nice homely feel about it. Food is available virtually the whole day; the dining room catering for full and more formal meals, and good bar snacks and lunches are served quickly and pleasantly in the lounge bar. Prices are moderate. Most bedrooms have private bathrooms and the usual modern appointments. High standards of comfort and service and a staff which seems anxious to meet the guest's every requirement.
Proprietors: Mr & Mrs H W McLean

WEIGH INN MOTEL
Burnside
Thurso KW71 4UG
Tel: 0847 63722

Outskirts of Thurso on A836 Scrabster road.
A busy 28 chalet motel overlooking the Pentland Firth and situated at the crossroads to the west coast of the Highlands and Scrabster, the sea port to the Orkneys. Guests return annually to enjoy the challenge of the Pentland Firth i.e. sea angling, surfing, wind surfing, water skiing etc. A spacious old world pub appropriately called The Bere and Byte offers pool, darts or watching sport on satellite TV and if your intentions are more serious there is a good range of interesting snacks, strong on home-cooking, available at lunchtime and in the evening. For those who prefer quieter surroundings the attractive cocktail bar makes a good setting for a more relaxed and enjoyable meal. All the self-catering chalets have private bath/shower rooms, colour TV, tea/coffee facilities. Who would expect to find petangue piste (French boules) in the very north of Scotland, and obviously very popular with visitors and locals alike. The only place of its type in the area, the Weigh Inn has a cared for and caring atmosphere.
Proprietor: Jim Youngson

TOMATIN

TOMATIN INN
Tomatin
Inverness-shire IV13 7YN
Tel: 08082 291

Off A9, 1 mile, halfway between Aviemore and Inverness.
This is a former farm steading, converted by the present proprietors into a country pub, with a friendly, relaxed atmosphere. Home-cooked bar meals are available in either the cosy 'locals' bar, with its colourful characters and open fire, or the lounge, with its more relaxed atmosphere and enclosed beer garden. The menu has been compiled with care; the food is imaginative and unusual, and very well presented. Meals are served at

lunchtime and during the evening. Dinner is served in the more intimate restaurant in the evening. Children are welcome and can safely play in the enclosed beer garden. A tour of the Tomatin Distillery, the largest independent distillery in the world, followed by a taste of its 10 year old malt at the local pub, is well recommended. It is well worthwhile to peel off the A9 to rest and enjoy this first class hostelry.
Proprietor: T Graeme Manson

TONGUE

BEN LOYAL HOTEL

Main Street
Tongue, By Lairg
Sutherland IV27 4XE
Tel: 0847 55 216

Tongue lies in the middle of the scenic north Sutherland coast at the junction of A838 from Durness and A836 from Lairg to John o'Groat's.

Tongue, from the Norse name Tunga meaning a spit of land, is a lovely part of Sutherland abounding in wildlife and with all sorts of sporting and recreational facilities available. The Ben Loyal is a delightful small hotel with, as its name suggests, splendid views to the mountain of that name and the Kyle of Tongue. There is a high standard of home-cooking and emphasis on fresh local produce wherever possible. Warm welcoming hospitality and a very friendly atmosphere throughout make this a very pleasant base either for a holiday in the area or as a stopping-off place.
Proprietors: Mel & Pauline Cook

TORPHICHEN

TORPHICHEN INN

The Square
Torphichen
By Bathgate
Tel: 0506 52826

Situated on the main road between Bathgate and Linlithgow.

It often comes as a surprise to the visitor to West Lothian to discover just how many historical connections are centred round the conservation village of Torphichen. Pride of place may go to the fine 12th century Torphichen Preceptory once the property of the Knights of St John but there are many other features of interest in and around the village. The Torphichen Inn, at the heart of the community, has been around in one form or another for several centuries. It is now a popular pub for both locals and visitors alike, with an attractive and comfortable lounge bar serving a good range of popular lunch and supper dishes. There is a special menu for children and vegetarians are also catered for. Prices are very modest. There is a special suite in which dinner dances are held on Fridays and Saturdays and there is a spacious public bar. There is a lot of atmosphere in this fine old village pub, and the staff are polite, quick and friendly.
Proprietors: J & M Robertson

TORTHORWALD

THE TORR HOUSE HOTEL

Torthorwald
Dumfries DG1 3PT
Tel: 038775214

A fine country house hotel overlooking the town with adequate parking and a very attractive children's play area with swings and a Mother Hubbard boot. The busy public bar is clearly a popular rendezvous for locals and nearby farmers and there is a charming little cocktail bar in addition to the lounge bar. The menu, wisely, is not too extensive but what it offers is good and the ample portions are well presented. There is an exciting range of sweets designed to tempt the most strong willed. Staff are welcoming and attentive. This would be a lovely place for a night out from Dumfries. Its outstanding situation, good food and pleasant atmosphere combine to create a sense of occasion. But equally it is a very good stopping-off place at any time for the visitor to the area.

Proprietor: Mrs Jean Pitt

TROON

PIERSLAND HOUSE HOTEL

Craig End Road
Troon
Ayrshire KA10 6HD
Tel: 0292 314747

Piersland House was built at the end of last century for Sir Alexander Walker of Johnnie Walker whisky fame. The hotel is just across the way from Royal Troon Golf Club. Apart from offering a good standard of food in its main dining room, the Piersland is well known locally for the quality of its bar menu. The Walker Lounge is luxuriously panelled in oak and original wood carvings and fireplaces, the design having been taken from a room in the Victoria and Albert Museum in London. It would be worth visiting this hotel just to experience the atmosphere of an age gone by, but you will also be impressed by the congenial and comfortable surroundings where the staff take great care in making your visit a pleasant one.

Proprietor: J A Brown

ULLAPOOL

MOREFIELD MOTEL & STEAKPLAICE RESTAURANT

North Road
Ullapool
Ross-shire IV26 2TH
Tel: 0854 2161

On north road leaving Ullapool immediately over small road bridge turn left 200 yards then turn into car park.

This low-slung modern building has undergone dramatic changes to its fortunes since being acquired by the partnership of its present owners, David Smyrl and David Marsh. Specialising in seafood its restaurant and indeed lounge bar menus are featured in many of the food guides. Situated a comfortable 10 minutes walk from the centre of the village – accessible by a footpath through the playing fields and crossing the local salmon pool. The bedrooms all en suite are well equipped and boast central heating, colour TV, tea/coffee facilities. Sample the hospitality and try the fresh seafood nearly always available. Then spend your evening chatting to the locals over 'a dram' – there are over 100 from which to choose. If you are in Ullapool this is well worth a visit. It has much to offer.

Proprietors: David Smyrl & David Marsh

UPHALL

HOUSTOUN HOUSE HOTEL

Uphall
West Lothian EH52 6JS
Tel: 0506 853831

Just off Edinburgh-Bathgate (A89) road at Uphall.

Houstoun House is a 16th century tower house standing in its own grounds. Within the old part of the building is the bar with its vaulted ceiling and stone floors. If you glance up you can still see the ceiling hooks which at one time may have hung hams or sides of beef. It is comforting on cold days to be greeted by a blazing fire in the enormous open fireplace, creating an atmosphere of warmth and conviviality. There is an excellent range of malt whiskies for the tasting and the cheerful and friendly staff will be only too happy to assist with your choice. A place with atmosphere for that relaxing drink perhaps before adjourning upstairs to sample the specialities of the dining room, which is renowned for its quality cuisine.

Proprietor: Gleddoch Hotels Ltd

WESTFIELD

THE LOGIEVALE INN

Westfield
West Lothian EH48 3BU
Tel: 0506 56088

Just off A801 junction 4 of M8 or M9, near Bathgate.

This old stone building promotes itself as the "pub/restaurant with traditional values" and the staff enthusiastically strive to provide the welcome and the standards this implies. You can meet the locals around the stove down in the bar, or relax in the lounge or restaurant by the glow of logs burning in the big stone fireplaces. A comfortable pub, with a cosy atmosphere in rustic surroundings. The quality of food is outstanding, with much attention to detail in presentation. A varied menu is available lunchtimes and evenings seven days a week. There is also an additional a la carte menu available at weekends, when it is advisable to book. This is a popular venue for business people, families and parties.

Proprietors: Iain & Georgina Shearer

WEST LINTON

THE LEADBURN INN

Leadburn
West Linton
Peeblesshire EH46 7BE
Tel: 0968 72952

Napoleon was only a boy, and Bonnie Prince Charlie still alive when, in 1777 the Leadburn opened its doors. Nothing keeps going for over 200 years unless it has something special to offer and so it is with the Leadburn. If John Buchan, the distinguished author who once ate there, were to call

again today he would be most impressed with the standard of the food, the unique railway carriage restaurant, the comfortable bedrooms, some with private bathrooms, and by the air of relaxed luxury. Bar snacks can be had all day seven days a week and in the evening the restaurant exploits to the full, the rich abundance of local fish, game and fresh produce in an interesting and worthy menu. Interestingly different.

Proprietor: Thomson Taverns

WHITBURN

CROFTMALLOCH INN

Longridge Road
Whitburn
West Lothian EH47 8HB
Tel: 0501 42318

A nice old farmhouse-style country inn with a well-kept car park and beer garden - and an inviting look to it. It is a sister establishment of the Hilcroft Hotel in Whitburn and under the same owner management. The bar lounge with lots of dark wood, beamed ceiling and lantern-style lighting is both attractive and comfortable. There is a menu of high standard fare with bar food available in the lounge and a separate restaurant for the more leisurely meal. The staff seem delighted to serve you. This is a first class pub restaurant with excellent food, high standards of service, good decor, and genuine hospitality.

Proprietors: John & Margaret Hilditch

WICK

MACKAY'S HOTEL
Union Street
Wick
Caithness KW1 5ED
Tel: 0955 2323

An old established Highland hotel well known to, and patronised by, the local business community but with an equally favourable reputation with the many visitors to this northern town. Mackay's does not have delusions of grandeur or pretend to be something it is not. What it is is a comfortable friendly hotel serving good food in pleasant surroundings and offering splendid value for money. The public areas are well kept and the hotel's 30 bedrooms all have private bathrooms and showers, colour TV etc. Centrally situated in the town, Mackay's is a convenient place to drop into for a bar lunch, a more formal meal, or indeed to use as a base from which to enjoy Caithness.
Proprietors: D J & D M Lamont

WISHAW

HARVIES
234 Main Street
Wishaw ML2 7HD
Tel: 0698 375546

The modern layout rather suggests a cafe bar but a lot of quality furniture and furnishing has gone into this acclaimed establishment which exudes an excellent atmosphere. It is a very popular lunchtime rendezvous particularly with professional people. Standards throughout are first class and staff respond to the surroundings by crisp, efficient and friendly service. Food is varied, of high quality and very reasonable in price. This is a really top class lounge bar where almost everyone will enjoy the atmosphere and the personal attention. An ideal town pub for food and drink. Live entertainment is an added attraction on most Thursday evenings.
Proprietor: Stakis plc

GUIDE TO PUBS OF TASTE IN SCOTLAND

INDEX   Page No

Abbey Court Restaurant, The: Elgin	53
Abbotsford, The: Edinburgh	40
Abernethy Hotel: Abernethy	12
Admiral, The: Glasgow	58
Albany Hotel: Edinburgh	40
Alexandria Hotel: Alexandria	12
Almondbank Inn: Perth	84
Anchor Hotel: Kippford	73
Aquila's Lounge Bar & Restaurant: Carluke	28
Archies (Stuart Hotel): East Kilbride	39
Ardencaple Hotel, The: Rhu	86
Ardlui Hotel: Loch Lomond	76
Arduthie Hotel: Crieff	31
Atholl Arms: Glasgow	58
Auchmithie Hotel: Auchmithie	14
Aulay's Bar: Oban	81
Auld Hoose, The: Edinburgh	40
Auld Hundred, The: Edinburgh	41
Auld Toll Tavern: Dunfermline	38
B J's Bar & Diner: Glasgow	58
Balcastle Hotel: Lochmaben	76
Balintore Hotel: Balintore	15
Balloch Hotel, The: Balloch	16
Balmoral Hotel: Moffat	78
Bank, The: Glasgow	58
Bank Inn: Rutherglen	87
Barmore Farm: Tarbert	98
Barn Bar, The: Oban	81
Barony Bar: Edinburgh	41
Beau Brummell: Edinburgh	41
Beechwood, The: Glasgow	59
Belfry, The: Glasgow	59
Bellevue Bar: Edinburgh	41
Ben Loyal Hotel: Tongue	100
Bianco's: Edinburgh	42
Birds and the Bees, The: Stirling	88
Black Bull, The: Mid Calder	78
Blackford Inn: Blackford	25
Blackness Inn: Blackness	25
Blackwater Inn, The: Glenshee	66
Blair Tavern, The: Auchintiber	14
Bobolovsky's Balloon: Glasgow	59
Bower Inn, The: Bower	27
Brabloch Hotel: Paisley	83
Brahan Seer: Inverness	68
Brasserie, The: Glasgow	59
Buchan Hotel, The: Ellon	54

Burnside Inn: Menstrie	78
Burrelton Park Hotel: Burrelton	28
Cafe Ca Va: Edinburgh	42
Cafe Ici: Aberdeen	11
Cafe Rogano: Glasgow	60
Cafe St James: Edinburgh	42
Caledonian Hotel: Lewis	75
Cambridge Bar: Edinburgh	42
Cameron's Inn: Aberdeen	11
Cardross Inn: Cardross	28
Carradale Hotel: Carradale	30
Castle Hotel, The: Stirling	97
Castlecary House Hotel: Castlecary	30
Cawdor Tavern, The: Cawdor	30
Cherry Tree Hotel: Coylton	31
Churchills: Aberdeen	11
Cleo's: Rosyth	86
Clouseau's: Elgin	54
Clovenfords Hotel: Clovenfords	30
Copper Tun: Livingston	75
Corn Exchange: Glasgow	60
Corner House Hotel: Montrose	79
Courtyard: Stirling	97
Covenanter Hotel, The: Falkland	55
Covenanters Inn: Nairn	80
Craigmonie Hotel: Inverness	68
Craignethan Hotel: Lesmahagow	74
Craigton Coach Inn: Monikie	79
Craw Inn, The: Eyemouth	55
Croftmalloch Inn: Whitburn	102
Cromarty Arms: Cromarty	32
Cross Keys Inn: Stonehouse	97
Crown & Cushion: Edinburgh	42
Crown Hotel: Portpatrick	85
Cuilfail Hotel: Kilmelford	72
Dark Island Hotel: Benbecula	25
Deacon Brodies: Edinburgh	43
Deerstalker Lounge Bar & Restaurant, The: Daviot East	33
Deil's Cauldron, The: Comrie	31
De Quincey's: Glasgow	60
Dip Inn, The (Mansion House Hotel): Elgin	54
Doctors, The: Edinburgh	43
Doublet Bar, The: Glasgow	60
Dow's: Glasgow	60
Duck Bay Hotel & Marina: Loch Lomond	76

Name	Page
Dykes, The: Stenhousemuir	88
Eglinton Arms Hotel, The: Eaglesham	39
Elizabethan, The: Dunfermline	38
Ensign Ewart: Edinburgh	43
Exchequer: Glasgow	61
Fairmile Inn, The: Edinburgh	43
Falls of Lora Hotel: Connel Ferry	31
Famous Peacock Inn, The: Edinburgh	44
Fernie Castle Hotel: Letham	74
Ferry Bridge Hotel: North Queensferry	80
Ferryhill House Hotel: Aberdeen	11
Finlay's: Glasgow	61
Finlay's: Inverness	68
Five Arches, The: Dumfries	35
Flemington Inn, The: Burnmouth	27
Fleshers Arms, The: Dumfries	35
Fordbank Country House Hotel: Bladnoch-By-Wigtown	26
Fox & Hounds: Houston	67
Garrick Bar: Edinburgh	44
Garvald Hotel: Garvald	57
George Bar, The: Hamilton	67
George Hotel, The: Inveraray	67
George Hotel: Thornhill	98
Glasgow Brasserie: Glasgow	61
Glen Mhor Hotel: Inverness	68
Glentanar, The: Aberdeen	11
Globe Inn: Dumfries	35
Gold Medal Tavern, The: Edinburgh	44
Gordon Hotel, The: Nigg	80
Granary, The: Glasgow	61
Greyfriars Bobby: Edinburgh	44
Grill, The: Aberdeen	12
Grosvenor Bar: Edinburgh	45
Grove Lounge: Thurso	99
Halfway House Hotel: Kingseat	72
Hamilton's: Paisley	83
Hanrahans: Glasgow	61
Harry's Bar: Edinburgh	45
Harvies: Paisley	83
Harvies: Wishaw	103
Haughdale Hotel: Inverness	69
Hawes Inn, The: South Queensferry	88
Haymarket, The: Edinburgh	45
Heathmount Hotel: Inverness	69
Herbs Wine Bar & Bouquet Garni Restaurant: Lochgoilhead	75
Hideaway, The: Dunfermline	38
Horsemill Inn: Denny	33
Houstoun House Hotel: Uphall	101
Hunter's Tryst: Edinburgh	45
Hunting Lodge, The: Kilmarnock	72
Inchmore Hotel: Inverness	69
Inn at Muckhart, The: Pool o' Muckhart	85
Innes Bar: Inverness	69
Inveroran Hotel: Bridge of Orchy	27
Inverpark Hotel: Arbroath	13
Irvine Arms/Geordies Byre: Drumoak	34
Izzy's Restaurant & Wine Bar (Lorne Tavern): Dollar	34
Justinlees Inn, The: Dalkeith	33
Kenilworth, The: Edinburgh	45
Kettlebridge Inn: Kettlebridge	71
Kilchrenan Inn: Kilchrenan	71
King's Arms Hotel: Girvan	58
Kinleith Arms: Edinburgh	46
Lady Ross Hotel: Ardgay	13
Last Drop, The: Edinburgh	46
Latheronwheel Hotel: Latheron	73
Leadburn Inn, The: West Linton	102
Le Cafe: East Kilbride	40
Lewiston Arms: Drumnadrochit	34
Liberton Inn: Edinburgh	46
Lochardil House Hotel: Inverness	70
Lochinvar Hotel: St Johns Town of Dalry	87
Loch Leven Hotel: Onich	82
Lock 27: Glasgow	62
Lodge on the Loch, The: Onich	82
Logievale Inn, The: Westfield	102
Longforgan Hotel, The: Longforgan	77
Longniddry Inn, The: Longniddry	77
Lord Lounsdale: Paisley	83
Lovat Arms Hotel: Beauly	16
Mackay's Hotel: Wick	103
Magnum, The: Edinburgh	47
Marchbank Hotel: Balerno	15
Marina Inn: Irvine	71
Marine Hotel: Stonehaven	97
Mariners Wine Bar (The Moorings): Fort William	56
Maxwell's: Glasgow	62
Maybury, The: Edinburgh	47
Merlin, The: Edinburgh	47
Minders Bar: Edinburgh	47
Mitre Bar, The: Glasgow	62
Moffat Arms, The: Ormiston	82
Morefield Motel & Steakplaice Restaurant: Ullapool	101

Muirtown Motel: Inverness	70
Murrayfield Hotel, The: Edinburgh	47
Napoleon's: Glasgow	62
National Hotel, The: Dingwall	34
Navaar House Hotel: Edinburgh	48
New Caledonian Hotel, The: Leven	74
Nicol's: Kirkcaldy	73
Nithsdale Hotel: Sanquhar	87
No 1, The: Dundee	37
North Kessock Hotel: North Kessock	81
Old Bank Bar: Dundee	37
Old Brewhouse, The: Arbroath	13
Old Howgate Inn, The: Penicuik	84
Old Inn, The: Carnock	29
Old Inn, The: Gairloch	57
Old Mill Inn, The: Blyth Bridge	26
Old Rome Farmhouse: Gatehead	57
PJ Clarke's: Edinburgh	48
Paddy's Bar: Edinburgh	48
Partick Tavern: Glasgow	62
Penguin Cafe, The: Edinburgh	48
Pentland Hotel: Thurso	99
Phoenix: Inverness	70
Piaf's Brasserie: Glasgow	63
Pier 39: Glasgow	63
Pierino's Ristorante & Cocktail Bar: Ayr	15
Piersland House Hotel: Troon	101
Pitfirrane Arms Hotel: Dunfermline	38
Place, The: Glasgow	63
Plockton Hotel: Plockton	85
Potarch Hotel: Banchory	16
Priory Hotel: Beauly	25
Pub, The: Edinburgh	49
Queen's Arms: Edinburgh	49
Queens Hotel: Dumfries	36
Queens Hotel: Gullane	66
Queensberry Hotel: Dumfries	36
Rabha's: Glasgow	63
Raeburn, The: Edinburgh	49
Ragazzi: Dumfries	36
Ramnee Hotel: Forres	56
Red Lion Inn & Restaurant, The: Prestwick	85
Red Lion Tavern: Fochabers	56
Riverside Inn, The: Ayr	15
Rock, The: Glasgow	64
Rosemount Golf Hotel: Blairgowrie	26
Rose Street Brewery: Edinburgh	49

Rotchell Hotel: Dumfries	36
Royal Archer, The: Edinburgh	49
Royal Hotel: Callander	28
Royal Hotel: Cromarty	32
Royal Hotel, The: Dysart	39
Royal Mile Tavern, The: Edinburgh	50
Runway Inn, The: Stoneywood	98
Rutland Hotel: Edinburgh	50
Salutation Inn: Montrose	79
Scaramouche: Glasgow	64
Scotts: Edinburgh	50
Sheep Heid Inn: Edinburgh	50
Ship Hotel: Eyemouth	55
Silver Broom: Perth	84
Skeabost House Hotel: Skye	87
Sloans: Glasgow	64
Smugglers Tavern: Arbroath	13
Starbank Inn & Restaurant: Edinburgh	51
Station Inn: Carluke	29
Steam Packet Inn, The: Isle of Whithorn	71
Stirling Arms: Dunblane	37
Stirling Castle Bar: Glasgow	64
Stonehouse Bar, The: Hamilton	67
Sun Inn, The: Dalkeith	33
Sutherland Arms Hotel: Golspie	66
Swan Inn, The: Eaglesham	39
Taste of Speyside, A: Dufftown	35
Tattler, The: Edinburgh	51
Telstar Public House & Restaurant: Old Kilpatrick	81
Thirty-Nine Steps, The: Glasgow	64
Three Barrels, The: Dundee	37
Three Tuns, The: Edinburgh	51
Thunderton House Hotel: Elgin	54
Tigh a Clachain: Mallaig	77
Times Square: Glasgow	65
Tomatin Inn: Tomatin	99
Tormaukin Inn: Glendevon	65
Torphichen Inn: Torphichen	100
Torr House Hotel, The: Torthorwald	100
Towie Tavern: Auchterless	14
Town House Hotel: Markinch	77
Trading Post, The: Edinburgh	51
Trading Post, The: Glasgow	65
Troqueer Arms: Dumfries	37
Tudor Hotel, The: Airdrie	12
Ubiquitous Chip: Glasgow	65
Victoria & Albert: Edinburgh	52
Vines Wine Bar (Gellions Hotel): Inverness	70

Wallace Cave: Lanark	73
Waterfront Wine Bar: Edinburgh	52
Wayfarers, The: Croftamie	32
Wee Bush Inn, The: Carnwath	29
Weigh Inn Motel: Thurso	99
West End Hotel: Fort William	57
Wheatsheaf Inn: Falkirk	55
Wheatsheaf Inn: Symington	98
Whighams, Wine Cellars: Edinburgh	52
Windsor Bar: Perth	84
Wine Glass, The: Edinburgh	52
Winking Owl, The: Aviemore	14
Woodside Hotel: Musselburgh	80
Worlds End Pub & Restaurant: Edinburgh	53
Ye Old Golf Tavern: Edinburgh	53
Ye Olde Inn: Edinburgh	53
Ye Olde Original Roslin Inn: Roslin	86

GUIDE TO PUBS OF TASTE IN SCOTLAND 1990

Editor in Chief
J M B MacMillan MBE MC

Editor
Nancy K Campbell BA

Design by
Apex Design

Printed in Scotland by
Mainsprint, Hamilton

Contributors
C H McMaster BA
Scottish Brewing Archive

Eric W Ridehalgh CMBII FSAE
Secretary SLTA

Published by
Taste of Scotland Scheme
Limited

The details quoted in this guidebook are as supplied to the publishers and to the best of the Company's knowledge are correct.
Neither The Scottish Licensed Trade Association nor the Taste of Scotland Scheme Limited accept any responsibility for any error or inaccuracy.

ISBN 1-871445-00-0

Taste of Scotland Scheme Limited 33 Melville Street Edinburgh EH3 7JF Telephone: 031 220 1900

NOTES